D1593549

FRANCIS SUAREZ
ON FORMAL AND UNIVERSAL UNITY

(De Unitate Formali et Universali)

MEDIAEVAL PHILOSOPHICAL TEXTS IN TRANSLATION
No.15

Marquette University Press

Milwaukee, Wisconsin

FRANCIS SUAREZ
ON FORMAL AND UNIVERSAL UNITY

(De Unitate Formali et Universali)

Translated from the Latin
With an Introduction

By
J. F. ROSS, Ph.D.
Assistant Professor of Philosophy
UNIVERSITY OF PENNSYLVANIA

MARQUETTE UNIVERSITY PRESS   MILWAUKEE, WIS.   1964

CONTENTS

Translator's Introduction

I. LIFE AND WORKS

Francis Suarez was born January 5, 1548 in Granada Spain. At the age of 10 he was tonsured, having elected an ecclesiastical career. For three and one half years he pursued literary studies and in the middle of his thirteenth year undertook the university course in civil and canon law, studies which made a permanent impression upon his mind. However, he interrupted his legal education by his decision to join the Society of Jesus, a decision greeted with doubt by representatives of the Order who thought his weak health and undistinguished record at law unpromising. Upon his insistence, he was allowed to enter the novitiate where, after three months, his maturity and virtue recommended his immediate transfer to Salamanca for training in philosophy. He was seventeen at the time. During two years of training in philosophy, his talents, urged by prodigious efforts to conquer a subject which seemed most difficult to him, earned him high repute. At nineteen he began theology and in 1570 with his studies completed, he commenced his teaching career. Although he taught philosophy only four years, as the normal prelude to teaching theology, and although the rest of his life was spent as professor of theology, he never ceased emphasizing the importance of philosophical knowledge as a prerequisite to theological learning: his *Metaphysical Disputations* were composed on this premise.

His forty-three years of preceptorship in theology met unusual recognition almost from the beginning. At the age of thirty-two he was given the chair in theology at the Jesuit College in Rome, the Order's most important college; his health prohibited his retaining this post for long and forced his return to Alcalà. In his forty-second year he published his first work: *De Verbo Incarnato,* a commentary of the third part of the *Summa Theologica* of St. Thomas. Shortly thereafter, Vasquez, a renowned Jesuit theologian who had been teaching in Rome, returned to Alcalà. Character disparity between these two good men caused Suarez to request transfer to Salamanca; later he moved to Coimbra where he spent twenty years amid a distinguished group of philosophers and theologians. In 1597, he published the *Metaphysical Disputations,* the significance of which is described below. In all, his published writings fill twenty-eight large volumes, one of the monuments of human intelligence and industry.

Over all, Suarez's life was a studious and quiet career of devoted teaching and debate, surrounded with an atmosphere of serious scholarship and scrupulous criticism. However, there were periods when

[1]

the acrimony of others and the intenseness arising from the importance of the matters debated could not have failed to produce great tension: for instance, the famous and somewhat strident debate among Fonseca, Bellarmine, Molina, Suarez and Banez over grace and predestination which ensued in a papal order that the disputants should desist; or, the period in which Banez selected an erroneous passage from Suarez's great work on Penance and secured from Pope Clement II a condemnation of the work until the passage should be corrected. For another brief period it seemed that Phillip II of Spain was trying to employ for political purposes an invitation for Suarez to teach in Portugal.

Shortly after the embarrassing incident of the condemnation, Suarez received compensating and supreme recognition when Pope Paul V bestowed the title *Doctor Eximius* upon him in appreciation for a paper: *De Immunitate Ecclesiastica A Venetiis Violata,* in which Suarez defended the rights of the Church in a serious dispute with the Venetian civil power. The last work published during Suarez's life was written in compliance with a request from the Papal Nuncio to Spain that Suarez assist in the intellectual dispute with the royal heretics in England. The *Defensio Fidei Catholicae Adversus Anglicanae Sectae Errores* defends both the indirect temporal power of the Pope and the right of citizens to overthrow a ruler turned tyrant. The English publicly burned the book in London, as did certain secularists in Paris.

Suarez died in Lisbon, September 28, 1617, where he had traveled to attempt rapprochement on a dispute between the Viceroy of Lisbon and the Holy See.

Suarez's works are:
  De Incarnatione Verbi, 1590.
  De Mysteriis Vitae Christi, 1592
  De Sacramentis, I, 1595
  Disputationes Metaphysicae, 1597
  Varia Opuscula Theologica, 1599
  De Sacramentis, II, 1602
  De Censuris, 1603
  De Deo Uno et Trino, 1606
  De Virtute et Statu Religionis, I, 1608
  De Virtute et Statu Religionis, II, 1609
  De Legibus, 1612
  Defensio Fidei Catholicae, 1613.

Posthumously published:
  De Gratia, I, III, 1619
  De Angelis, 1620

[2]

De Opera Sex Dierum, 1621
De Anima, 1621
De Fide, Spe et Caritate, 1621
De Virtute et Statu Religionis, III, 1624
De Virtute et Statu Religionis, IV, 1625
De Ultimo Fine, 1628
De Gratia, II, 1651
De Vera Intelligentia Auxilii Efficacis, 1655
Opuscula Sex Inedita, 1859 (which, as the title indicates, contains
    material whose exact status and place in Suarez's work is yet
    to be determined).
Some four volumes of manuscript material have not as yet been
    published.

The Disputation presented here is taken from the two, thousand-paged, double-columned volumes which comprise the *Metaphysical Disputations*. It is a fair sample of the erudition, objectivity, and devotion to a new scholasticism firmly joined to the tradition of Western philosophy which characterizes the entire work. No one can deny that Suarez is somewhat laborious and diffuse and even, sometimes, confusing in his style; but neither can anyone deny that his painstaking statement of the views held by others on every problem he treats has the wonderful advantage of setting his own views clearly in the perspective of his time.

Although one must be cautious concerning the applicability of much of Suarez's discussion of universals to the current of twentieth century analytically-oriented discussion of this problem, one need not qualify his admiration of Suarez's achievement, especially when it is viewed in terms of the stages to which the problem had been advanced in his time. Moreover, even though our extensive current literature on universals[1] has the appearance of even greater clarity and precision, it is yet to be satisfactorily established that any further progress has been made toward a solution or even that the problem is really any better understood or better stated now than it was by the Doctor Eximius in the Silver Age of Scholasticism.

---

[1] See, for instance, Bertrand Russell "On the Nature of Universals and Particulars," in *Logic and Knowledge*, edited by Robert C. Marsh, (Allen and Unwin, 1956), p. 103; and the essays by Bochenski, Church and Goodman in *The Problem of Universals; A Symposium* (South Bend: University of Notre Dame Press, 1956), and W. Van Orman Quine, *From a Logical Point of View* Harvard: 1953; and *Word and Object* (Cambridge: 1960); P. F. Strawson, Massachusetts Institute of Technology Press, *Introduction to Logical Theory* (New York: Wiley, 1952), and "Singular Terms, Ontology, and Identity," *Mind* LXV, (1956), 433-54.

II. METHOD

The modern reader may have some difficulty following the course of argument in this disputation, first because of its complexity and secondly because Suarez urges the arguments of his opponents at great length, even supplying them with "confirmations" which they themselves never thought of. Then, in rejecting their views, he dismantles them "board by board," often arguing against each premise of each argument. After this complex preparation, he gives his own view with as many demonstrative arguments and probabilistic supporting considerations as he can find. Furthermore, since he divided this disputation into eleven sections (in several of which the whole didactic apparatus is employed) some of which deal with several different phases of a problem, only attentive reading will permit one to appreciate the careful architectonic of the disputation.

The general pattern displayed in most sections is this: (a) a statement of the problem in its various interpretations (sometimes accompanied by a list of *possible* views); (b) a statement of various solutions given by important philosophers; (c) supporting arguments for the opinions of these philosophers; (d) minute destruction of opinions Suarez rejects; (e) statement and support of the true or most probable opinion.

This format is further complicated by the *formal* argument which is often employed. That is, after an expanded and informal statement of a view, Suarez often "reduces it to form" and "replies in form": he puts the view in *syllogistic* form and follows certain rules in replying to it. Briefly the rules of reply are: (a) Do not deny the major premise; only a fool uses a false major premise and politeness demands that such an argument be ignored; nor should one reject an argument as formally invalid, for the same reason. (b) If the minor premise is false, then deny it, show it is false and proceed to deny the conclusion. (c) If the minor premise needs to be *distinguished* (that is, if two or more senses can be assigned it), make the distinction, and make a corresponding distinction in the conclusion. (d) If the major premise needs to be distinguished, do so; then "counter-distinguish" the minor (that is, show that it trades on the double-meaning of the major) and proceed to deny that the conclusion follows. Often, when Suarez presents a formal argument for his own view, he leaves the conclusion unstated, since the context supplies it.

As he appears in the *Disputation on Formal and Universal Unity*, Suarez will, no doubt, be called an "eclectic"; but it would be absurd to mean this pejoratively, or to think that Suarez selected unimaginatively and unoriginally among the views of his predecessors and contemporaries. Suarez, here as everywhere in the *Disputationes*, is cre-

[4]

ating a new systematic metaphysics which has much indeed to recommend it as a rival to St. Thomas and Duns Soctus, and even to Aristotle; and no one does him a service to call him a Thomist or align him too closely with any other thinker, whether small or great.

III. THE TEXT

Since there is no complete critical edition of Suarez's works, we were forced to make our translation from the most recent complete edition, *Opera Omnia*, 26 vols., (Paris: Vives, 1856-66), the edition to which citations are most frequently made. Other printings of the collected works were at Mainz and Lyons (1630), at Venice (1740), and at Besançon (1856-62).

There is no scholarly dispute over the authenticity of this Disputation or over the substantial integrity of the text. However, some bibliography may be of assistance to readers with special interests:

1. C. Sommervogel, S.J., *Bibliothèque de la Compagnie de Jésus,* 9 vols, (Paris: Alphonse Picard, 1890-1900). One will find a list of the various editions of Suarez's works here.

2. R. de Scorraille, S.J., *Francois Suarez de la Compagnie de Jésus,* 2 vols, (Paris: Lethiellieux, 1912-13). This is the best credited of the biographies. An English popularization is: J. H. Fichter, S.J., *Man of Spain: Francis Suarez* (New York: Macmillan, 1940).

It is my opinion that there is no reliable secondary source on Suarez's doctrine on universals and that most of the charges of "nominalism" made against Suarez are entirely irresponsible. However, one might study: J. M. Alexandra, *La Gnoseologia del Doctor Eximio y la acusasión nominalista* (Comillas: Stantander, 1948); and, perhaps: J. Hellin, *La Analogia del ser y el conocimiento de Dio en Suarez* (Madrid: 1947).

IV. THE PRINCIPLE DOCTRINES CONTAINED IN THIS WORK

In the following pages we shall: (e) Summarize the chief doctrines of the disputation. (b) Explain several technical and subtle points in the arguments. (c) Make some comparisons to other well-known writers on the problem.

1) As Suarez understood the long medieval controversy over universals, the chief positions were held by: (a) Aquinas and his followers: Cajetan, Capreolus, Soncinas, Ferrara, Javellus, and Soto; (b) Scotus and his followers: Francis of Mayronnes, Lychetus, and Antonius Andreas; and (c) Occam and certain "nominalists": Marsilius of Inghen, Albert of Saxony, Adam Wodeham, and Peter Aureolis (Suarez's opinion is in many respects startlingly like that of Peter). He also recognizes certain fringe positions such as those of Durandus,

Henry of Ghent, and Giles of Rome. None of these authors denies the proposition that there are some mind-dependent entities which are universal, namely, concepts or ideas. They all agree that a universal term (like "red," "tall," "colored," "dog," "man") refers to or signifies *both* concepts which are mind-dependent and other things which are not. Moreover, they all agree that the mode of reference or kind of signification by which the term refers to a concept is different from that by which it refers to the real things. The basis of *disagreement* among the authors is this: some things which are not mind-dependent but are found *in rerum natura* or *in re ipsa,* or *a parte rei* are said to be universals by some and are denied that status by others; and the expression "X is universal but not mind-dependent" does not have the same meaning for all these writers.

2) When Suarez asks himself the question: "What things are there which are universal?" he replies that there are *two* sorts of things which are universal: (a) concepts or some mind-dependent things known technically as *entia rationis;* (b) those things independent of the operations of the mind, *entia realia,* which are *denominated* universals.

Since he grants that all things which exist independently of the operations of the mind must be singular or individual,[2] he argues that "being universal" is not an *intrinsic* property of anything which is not a concept, and, hence, the universals *in re* are not separate from or really different from the singulars; rather, things independent of the mind can be correctly called universals only through *denominatio extrinsica.* This, he says, is obvious, since the nature which John has is not *communicable* (disposed to be in or shared by many things) as it exists in John, but only as it is conceived by some mind. Hence "is actually a universal" is a property which certain concepts alone have intrinsically; and *Universals* are natures which have been made actually communicable through the operations of the intellect. The nature of any given singular is, prior to the consideration thereof by the mind, only analogously and potentially universal, in that it is the potential subject or *materia circa quam* of the universalizing operations of the mind. The nature of a thing is communicable to other things only in the sense that it is not logically impossible for something else to exist which is enough like the first to be conceived of *via* the same concept. The form in the mind is actually universal while the form in the individual is individuated along with the individual; and the for-

---

[2] D.5, passim. It should be noted that all references are to the Paris edition of the *Opera Omnia* of 1856-66. Henceforth, citations of the *Dispu-* *tationes Metaphysicae* will be made as follows: D___,S___,N___, where 'D' refers to the disputation, 'S' to the section and 'N' to the number.

mal unity of the individual essence is multiplied as often as the individuals are: so, the form existing in any individual is at most potentially universal, as potentially the subject of that abstraction by which the mind forms for itself a concept, a mental species, which adequately represents many individuals.[3]

Suarez denies that there are any actual universals independent of the mind and agrees with Averroes: "Intellectus facit universalitatem in rebus," and with St. Thomas "intentionem universalitatis esse ab intellectu" (*Ia*,q85,a.1); for he says: "If 'universal in being' means that which is universal in the thing itself, there is no universal of this kind. . . ."

When he says the form of this particular individual, John, is potentially universal, he does not mean, as some medievals did, that this form, found in John, is communicable or capable of being shared by many individuals in some literal sense of "sharing."[4] Nor does he mean that the form or nature found in John is potentially universal in the sense that it has or might have some (literal) community throughout many things, which serves as a basis for the abstraction by which the intellect renders the form universal and predicable of many individuals (the position ascribed to Scotus). The form in an individual, John, is potentially universal only in the sense that the form can become *actively* a partial cause of a concept which is truly universal and through which some agent can apprehend or grasp the essence of John as well as the essences of other things like John.

In brief, Suarez claims: (1) that nothing is *actually* and intrinsically universal which is not mind-dependent; (2) that the forms of individual things are potentially universal only in so far as those forms can be abstracted and rendered by the mind "universales in representando," universal in their representative function. Yet Suarez also states that universals, *quoad rem denominatam,* are real: "Res quae universales denominatur, vere in re existunt";[5] a statement which may seem inconsistent with the position that actual and intrinsic universals are "beings of reason" and with his *denial* of the Scotist view that a nature, denominated universal, but existing in singulars has of itself the sort of unity which would place potential *universality* or true community in reality besides in the mind. However, the conflict is only

---

[3] It is important to remember that Suarez subscribes to the Aristotelean view that the form in the mind, i.e., the concept, is the *same* form as is found in the thing and that there is a causal relation between the form in the thing and the mind's conceiving (but one of formal causality).

[4] "Aptitudo ad existendum in multis non est aliqua proprietas realis conveniens naturae communi secundum se ante operationem intellectus.' D6, S4,N6.

[5] D6,S2,N1.

prima facie and an understanding of the notion of "denomination," not explained here by Suarez, renders the statement in question quite innocuous.

3) *Denomination*—Aristotle in the *Categories*,[6] speaks of terms used "derivatively" (as the Edghill translation puts it): "Thus the grammarian derives his name from the word 'grammar' and the courageous man from the word 'courage'." This term, "derivatively" (Greek: παρωνομως) was translated into Latin as *denominative*, "denominatively."

A term "t" is used denominatively, according to the developed usage of the notion in the thirteenth and later centuries, when it is employed in discourse about something, x, which derives its legitimate bearing of the term "t" not from its own nature but from its relation to something else, y, which does bear "t" legitimately because of its own nature. Aquinas' theory of analogy of attribution was designed to explain the foundations for just such legitimate transfers of terms with accompanying morphological changes in many cases. And it is just such a relation of analogy of attribution which explains the relation of the property and quality senses of terms like "red," etc.

The idea that we refer to a group of things with a term primarily used of something else but extended in scope because of the relation of the first group to the second, is very old in the history of philosophy, being the basis for the long tradition which includes the PROS EV analogy of Aristotle and the analogy theories of the Arabians, Alexander of Hales, Albert the Great, Aquinas, Sylvester of Ferrara, Cajetan, and Suarez himself. All these theories involved a distinction of "primary" and "secondary" usages of a term, where the meaning of the term in former use was part of the meaning of the term as it occurred in its latter use.

Some reference to St. Thomas will, perhaps, make the concept of extrinsic denomination clearer and will show how the designation of the nature, as it is found existing independently of the mind, as "universal," is a designation by analogy of attribution.

St. Thomas says[7] that anything or group of things related, even variously, to one common thing can be characterized by terms primarily applicable to the one, but extended to the others because of the relation which obtains. He says also:

---

[6] Ch 1, 1a, line 13.

[7] IIIa,q.6,a.1, corpus: omnia quae habent ordinem ad unum aliquid, licet diversimode, ab illo denominari possunt; sicut a sanitate, quae est in animali, denominatur sanum non solum animal, quod est sanitatis subjectum, sed dicitur medicina sana, in quantum est sanitatis effectiva; dieta, vero inquantum est conservativa ejusdem et urina, in quantum est significativa ipsius.

[8]

There are two ways in which something is predicated denominatively. It may be denominated by that which is *outside* it, as when something is said to be "somewhere" on account of its place and "sometime" on account of a time; also, something can be denominated by that which is *in it,* as something is said to be white from whiteness; but a thing is not found to be denominated, as it were, from something *outside* it when it is denominated on account of some relation, but rather from something *inhering* in it; for someone is not denominated "father" except on account of the paternity which is present in him.[8]

Examples of extrinsic denomination of the first sort are: "my childhood companion," "my Ann Arbor colleague," "my onetime assistant," etc. Also in *De Veritate:*

> A thing is denominated with reference to something else in two ways. (1) It occurs when the very reference itself is the meaning of the denomination. Thus urine is called healthy with respect to the health of the animal. For the meaning of "healthy" as predicated of urine is: "serving as a sign of the health of the animal." In such cases what is relatively denominated does not get its name from a form inherent in it but from something extrinsic to which it is referred. A thing is denominated by reference to something else when the reference is not the meaning of the denomination but the cause. For instance, air is said to be bright from the sun, not because the very fact that the earth is referred to the sun is the brightness of the air, but because the placing of the air directly before the sun is the cause of its being bright.[9]

Both the denominations described in the above are *extrinsic,* i.e., based upon the external relation of the thing we are talking about to something else. The passage from the *Contra Gentiles* clearly distinguishes between *extrinsic* and *intrinsic* denomination, the latter being based upon a form present in the thing denominated, the former supposing no such thing. Intrinsic denomination may be ignored in this context, since Suarez explicitly denies that there can be any real property of universality intrinsic in the natures which are independent of the mind. Instead, he says that natures outside the mind are universal by extrinsic denomination. And although he does not here subdivide extrinsic denomination into the two kinds described by St. Thomas in *De Veritate,* as quoted above, it is abundantly clear

[8] Duplex est modus quo aliquid denominative praedicatur. Denominatur enim ab eo quod *extra* ipsum est, sicut a loco dicitur alquas esse alicubi et a tempore, aliquando; aliquid vero denominatur ab eo quod *inest,* sicut ab albedine, albus; a relatione vero non invenitur aliquid denominari quasi exterius existente, sed inhaerente; non enim denominatur alquis pater, nisi a paternitate quae ei inest. C.G.2, 13. Also: Ia-IIae, q. 113,a.1; IIIa,q.22,a.6; 3 Physic,5,1; 5 Physic,8e; and De Veritate, q.21,a.4 ad 2; Translation by Robert W. Schmidt, S.J. (Chicago: Regnery, 1954), under English title: *Truth.*

[9] *De Veritate,* q.21,a.4.

that the nature in the individual is universal in the first manner: by extrinsic denomination based upon and logically following upon the relationship between the nature in the particular thing and the formal concept in the mind.

The apparently mysterious relation of "extrinsic denomination" is thus seen to be explicable as a kind of secondary reference where the same term is used to refer to both the thing which has the property primarily signified by that term and to the things related in various ways to something's having the property signified by that term. To refer to a thing by extrinsic denomination is, in most cases, to employ a term which is analogous according to the rule of attribution. Thus, there is a strong similarity in the analogy by which someone says of a certain design: "My, that's a fine ship," even though the design is only on paper, a design described here in terms of its formal effect, and the analogy by which one says that the form of the individual is universal, even though it is the form of a particular, because of one of its formal effects, the content of the concept which is actually universal.

When Suarez talks of the things which are denominated universals, he is not, as should now be evident, talking about things which have any intrinsic property of universality or even communicability (which he thinks is entailed by universality), but rather of things which are called universal because of the causal relation they have to the form in the intellect which is truly universal in that through the one form many individuals are apprehended. The form in the thing is universal only because it can be the objective concept (the thing-as-conceived) which corresponds and causally determines the formal concept (the conception-of-the-thing), which is universal. To state Suarez's position in Thomist terms, the form of the individual is universal, but the term "universal" is not univocal with its use in expressions of the form "the form in the intellect is universal"; rather, the two uses of "universal" are related according to analogy of attribution, where the causal relation of the primary analogate (the concept) and the secondary analogate (the form in the individual) is one where the form of the individual is formal cause of the content of the idea.[10]

In its most general outline, this is the position of Suarez on the metaphysical status of universals.

4) This metaphysical doctrine is succinctly and clearly stated in Section 5 (pp. 70-73 of this translation). Apart from the explanations

---

[10] However, Suarez explicitly provides that the formal cause of the *universality* of the formal concept is the intellect and not the form in the thing; the efficient cause is the mind conceiving and the nature, qua universal, is at best *materia circa quam.*

given above and an extended explanation of the important "distinction *ex natura rei*" (which follows) no detailed commentary is strictly necessary to aid Suarez's own explanation of his adherence to the moderate realist formula *"formaliter in mente, fundamentaliter in re."* However, it is interesting to note that in this passage, Suarez appropriates for himself several very common and powerful medieval arguments as to why the nature in a particular man, Peter, cannot be actually universal and cannot even be potentially universal (in the sense that numerically the same form *could* be shared by another); the only alternative appeared to be that the form in the individual is *fundamentally* universal. And, of the various possible interpretations of this phrase, Suarez chooses the one mentioned earlier, that the universality of the form is an extrinsic denomination and that in the same way, the form is fundamentally communicable; it is communicable only in the sense that there is nothing about the form of any individual which is such that it would be impossible for anything else to be like it in essential respects, and by which it is impossble that some other individual could be known or thought about by means of the same formal concept.[11]

In a word, the *fundamentum in re* of universality: "solum est non-repugnantia in ipsis etiam individuis ut habere possent alia sibi similia."[12] Suarez clearly thinks this is all that is required on the part of the object for the possibility of universal concepts. For, given the nature of the intellect, it follows that the form in the individual is capable of determining the content of a concept which can serve as medium of cognition for further things.

The "distinction *ex natura rei*," mentioned by Suarez in the key passage cited above is one of the most subtle points of the disputation, especially since there are several senses in which it is employed. Moreover, it is the fundamental concept in Suarez's dispute with Scotus, a dispute which underlies the whole disputation. For Suarez had no difficulty, using Occam's arguments, in dismissing the extreme realist view of Plato and he had no interest in extreme nominalist views like that attributed to Roscellinus by Anselm. But Scotus, who is apparently less moderate and more realist than St. Thomas, Avicenna, or Aristotle, posed a definite problem both on the nature of formal unity and on the foundation in reality for universal concepts.

5) *Suarez Disputes Scotus*—Scotus thinks that the formal unity of the common nature is independent of the considerations of the mind and is distinct from and different from numerical unity, not merely by reason of what the mind *does*, but because of something in the constitution of things independently of any consideration thereof by

---

[11] D6,S5,N3.   [12] D6,S5,N3.

the mind. Suarez, on the contrary, thinks that the formal sameness of things is entirely accounted for by the *distinguishing mind,* which is, when it conceives entitative unity, attending to differences in individuals, and which is, when it conceives essential unity, attending to differences in *kinds* of things.

Further, Scotus thinks there is only one formal unity which belongs to human nature; this unity is *not* multiplied in number with the multiplication of individuals which share human nature: there is one form or essence in all humans, although the form is particularized in each. The formal unity of human nature is not the result of the fact that the individuals are *not* distinguished with respect to "kind" by the mind, but is rather the result of a unity which belongs to the common nature independently of the mind's operations, which belongs to the natures prior to their individuation in things and which *determines* or accounts for the indistinguishibility of the particulars (with respect to essence) by the mind.

The Thomists and Suarez, on the other hand, think that there is a kind of unity (for instance, in the *essence* which all men share) which is distinguished by the *mind* from the numerical unity of individual things; this formal unity is multiplied with the individual unities; there are as many formal unities as there are forms.[13] The fact that the mind *fails* to distinguish various particulars as to essence is the basis of our thinking them to share a common nature; for the essence of each (the formal unities of each) must be similar, otherwise such a distinction of essence *would* have been made.[14] But Aquinas and Suarez see no need to suppose that (or way of explaining how) there is something (the common nature) real but not existent which is independent of the distinguishing mind, which is actually found in several things and which accounts for the fact that the mind finds groups of particulars indistinguishable in essence, as Scotus maintans.

Suarez holds that things are said to be of the same nature because their forms are similar to such a degree that these things can be known (i.e., apprehended) through the same formal concept; whereas, Scotus thinks things are said to be of the same nature because they actually share something, which though it does not exist, is yet *real* and is found entirely in each thing which shares it.[15]

13 D6,S1,N11.
14 The notion of "similarity" is discussed below in paragraph 6.
15 Suarez (D6,S1,N2) mentions attempts to mitigate differences between Thomas and Scotus by saying that they may not really differ; for what St. Thomas calls a "distinction of reason," Scotus called a "formal distinction"; and what Thomas called a "congruence or similarity," Scotus called "unity." This, however, is not quite correct; for there is a significant difference between a distinction of reason which depends for its actuality upon the operations of the mind and a formal distinction which obtains independ-

Suarez discusses the Scotist opinion at some length since the status of the "common nature" plays a crucial role in the discussion of universals. For if Scotus could establish his contention that there must be common natures, independent of the distinguishing mind and shared by all the particulars of a given essence, then he could easily maintain his thesis that the potential universal, the *universale in re* independent of the mind and found in things, is the common nature which things of the same essence share. This is precisely the form of realism which Suarez wants to discredit.

Suarez, attempting to refute the Scotist view and establish his own, employs several arguments, the consideration of which brings out their subtle disagreement. He maintains that: (1) all the philosophers are agreed that each thing has only one essence and that in each thing there is, therefore, that lack of essential division which is called "essential unity"; (2) that the essential or formal unity and the individual or numerical unity of any given thing are distinct, at least mentally, since they can be distinguished logically and since the necessary conditions for the one are not the same as the necessary conditions for the other. But, he insists, there is in a particular thing (say, a man) nothing which accounts for such a distinction if we ignore the operations of a conceiving mind. He argues as follows:

(a) Given Aristotle's premise: *destructis primis substantiis, impossible est aliquid remanere,* the common nature considered in itself is not a real thing and has no reality apart from the individuals in which it is found; therefore it is only mentally distinct.

This, of course, is a moot point. Scotus admits that if the individuals are destroyed, so also is the common nature and the universal.[16] But Scotus, as we shall explain below, clearly holds that *non-separable* realities may be distinct *a parte rei* and independently of the mind's operations. Hence, there is nothing in the first argument which militates against Scotus' position unless one reads Scotus in terms of Suarez's doctrine of distinctions, as will be explained.

(b) Using another traditional premise, Suarez argues that since whatever is intrinsic and essential to a thing is not distinct from that thing (apart from distinctions imposed by the mind), the formal unity which is both intrinsic and essential to any thing is not distinct from the thing. Again Scotus would counter with: "I distinguish the major: separably distinct? Granted. Inseparable but really distinct? Not granted."[17]

---

ently of any consideration of the mind. Suarez was not satisfied with this arbitration.

[16] *Met.*, VII,q13, n23 (Vol. 7, 424); "Potest enim et universale corrumpi ab actu esse, corruptis omnibus singularibus." See also: *Rep.* II, d3, q1,n5; *Ox.*II,d3,q7,n4.

[17] I mention Scotus' quite certain replies to these two arguments to show

[13]

Suarez concluded from those two arguments that formal unity, in so far as it is really found in things prior to their consideration by the intellect, is not common to many things; rather there are as many formal unities as there are individuals: "tot multiplicari unitates formales quot sunt individua."

Moreover, Suarez argued that the formal unity of one individual cannot be shared by any other, since the formal unity of the first is lost with the destruction of the first, while that of the second is independent of the existence of the first. This is what Suarez means by saying that the formal unity of the individual is not communicable; and so also, the essence or nature of the individual (as it exists *a parte rei* and independently of thought) is also incommunicable, a conclusion opposed to Scotus.[18]

6) *Similarity*—Suarez says:

Thus it follows from these facts, first that although each individual is formally one *a parte rei* and apart from the consideration of the mind, nevertheless, several individuals which are said to be of the same nature are not one reality with a true unity which is in the things, but are merely a unity which is to be found fundamentally in the things or as a result of the intellect. . . . Secondly, it follows that it is one thing to speak of formal unity and another thing entirely to speak of the community of that unity; for the unity is in the things, as has been said; however, the community, properly and strictly speaking, is not in the things, since no unity found in reality is common, as we have shown; but there is in things a certain similarity in their formal unities, on which the community which the intellect can attribute to such a nature as conceived by it, is based; this similarity is not properly unity since it does not imply the undividedness of the entities on which it is based but merely implies their agreement or their relation or the co-existence of both.[19]

In effect, things are said to be of the same nature if what confers formal unity (their essences) be sufficiently similar. But what is the criterion of *sufficient* similarity and what is involved in the notion of

how very important the "formal distinction *a parte rei*" really is to the position of Scotus and how he calls things which are formally distinct, "distinct *ex natura rei*," whereas Suarez so designates only really or modally distinct things.

[18] Duns Scotus: *Opus Oxoniense* (herein cited as *Ox*): *Ox*. II,d3,q1,n10: Communitas convenit naturae extra intellectum, et similiter singularitas. Et communitas convenit ex se naturae, singularitas autem convenit naturae per aliquid in re contrahens ipsum; sed universalitas non convenit rei ex se, et ideo concedo quod quaerenda est causa universalitatis, non tamen quaerenda est causa communitatis alia ab ipsa natura; et posita communitate in ipsa natura secundum propriam entitatem et unitatem, necessario oportet quaerere causam singularitatis, quae superaddit aliquid illi naturae cujus est.

[19] D6,S1,N12.

"similarity" itself, if it excludes "having something in common" in any literal sense?

Suarez considers a somewhat similar question, in terms of an objection to his theory which might be raised, especially by a Scotist:

> Someone will insist that since the fact that several individuals can be multiplied under the same species does not arise from the intellect but is founded in the nature of the case, then the disposition to be in many things accrues to the nature of itself and not from the intellect. The inference is obvious, for these two are either the same or follow one another in reality, namely: that individuals can be multiplied under the same species and that the specific nature can be communicated to them.[20]

His reply to the difficulty is:[21] (1) The antecedent is correct; the fact that things can be multiplied alike in species is indeed found in the things themselves and is not derived from the operations of the mind. (2) However, the consequent that the disposition to be in many things accrues to the nature of itself, must be distinguished. For in one sense, the inference fails; namely, if we interpret the consequent to mean that there is required some disposition on the part of the nature apart from the contracting differences required for individuation and actualizable through those differences. For, he says, such a disposition is not required; all that is required is that there should not be essential to the nature as it is found in any individual, any property which would make it impossible for anything else to be like that thing in nature. "Nam in multiplicatione individuorum ejusdem speciei non est in re alia communicatio naturae quam assimilatio et convenientia quaedam inter ipsa individua." Suarez by analyzing the notion of similarity apart from any reference to actual community of properties or forms, circumvents Scotus, as he interprets him.

He also considers the following objection to his assertion that the unity of the universal is not prior to or independent of the operations of the mind.

> Perhaps it may be said that one finds in reality not only that formal unity by which each human nature, for example, is said to be formally one in itself, but one also finds the unity by which all human natures are said to have the same formal structure, and consequently a formal unity by reason of which they share the same definition and all men are said to be *a parte rei* of the same nature.[22]

Suarez replies: "Sed contra, nam, haec revera non est unitas sed similitudo tantum"—this is not unity, it is likeness.

[20] D5,S4,N12.
[21] D6,S4,N13.
[22] D6,S2,N13.

For there is nothing both one and in fact undivided in reality in this and in that human nature; but there is merely in this, something to which something is similar in that other nature. Yet this is not real unity, but similarity. In this sense only, several things can be said to be of the same nature *a parte rei*, that is, of similar nature: for this identity, since it is said to obtain among distinct things cannot be anything in reality other than a similarity by reason of which they are said to share or to have the same definition, fundamentally in virtue of the mentioned similarity, but formally through reason, for definition is the work of reason.[23]

Moreover, Suarez points out that the actual likeness of things is not part of the notion of a universal since there could be universals even if there were no existents.

Although he did not explain what is implied by a correct assertion that two things are alike or similar, he clearly did not feel that for two things, A and B, to be alike there must be some third thing which is a "part of" or proper to both, like an umbrella over the heads of two people. On the contrary, this is exactly what he denied. He insists that for two things to be alike, they must be such that they can be conceived through the same formal concept; and he *seems* to think that the "fundamental" sameness consists in the tendency of the two things to cause in us the same formal concept, while the formal sameness or similarity of two things consists precisely in the fact that, being conceived through the same formal concept, they receive the same definition:

> Several individuals which are said to be of the same nature are not one reality with a true unity which is in the things, but are merely a unity which is fundamentally in the things, or in the things through the operation of the intellect.[24]

In brief, two things are fundamentally alike only if they would give rise to the same formal concept, and they are formally alike only if they have been given the same definition or have been conceived through one concept.

It is perfectly compatible with Suarez's doctrine to say that the formal concept of a nature, once formed, can be recalled by the appearance of a sufficiently similar impressed species, and that as a result, the various individuals conceived at different times do in fact give rise to numerically the same formal concept, via this storage and recall of concepts. Suarez's writings, however, do not clearly and unequivocally present such a theory. Furthermore, there seems to be no reason for saying that he is committed to such a view, since, he might have held that the concepts produced by the same thing conceived at differ-

---

[23] *Ibid.*   [24] D6,S1,N12.

ent times are not numerically the same but are specifically the same; of course, to say the latter would require some additional criterion of the sameness of concepts, and no such criterion is offered by Suarez. He is simply not specific enough about what determines the sameness of concepts.

Regardless of which explanation of the sameness of concepts (i.e., numerical or specific) Suarez would have accepted or of whether he would have proposed some third alternative, it is evident that a sufficient condition for its being the case that two things are formally the same is that they have been conceived or apprehended through the same formal concept.

It should now be evident that Suarez and Scotus, while agreeing that formal universality is found only in concepts, disagree radically about the *fundamentum in re*. Because Suarez thinks that the distinction of formal and numerical unities is mind-dependent (a distinction of reason) and because he thinks that the notion of "common formal nature" is *logically posterior* to that distinction, it follows that "common form" is mind-dependent and is not a real characteristic of the things but is merely *attributed* by *extrinsic denomination* to the things. Scotus thinks unity and community are intrinsic and real characteristics of the nature found in the individuals.

Suarez explicitly and adamantly claimed that the community of the common nature, *qua* common, is not something independent of the mind; the common nature is common in the same way in which it is universal—by extrinsic denomination; in fact, the nature in *Peter* is said to be *common* by extrinsic denomination, by our attributing to it a causal relation to a property which really belongs to the concept "man." He said: "the disposition to exist in many things is not some real property belonging to the common nature by itself apart from the operation of the understanding."[25] Just as explicitly and adamantly, Scotus said: "Community accrues to the nature outside the intellect, and so does singularity."[26] Scotus, definitely taking a different initial stance on the problem from that of Suarez, supposes at the outset that there is a real community in the natures of things, a community which is wholly independent of our perceptions. This is not to be causally explained since it is a logical consequence of the possibility of a nature. Rather it is to serve as a *principle* of explanation; for one cannot even speak of the singularity of things without supposing the possibility of community. Instead, both the singularity of things and the universality of things are in need of causal explanations.

It is on this question of the relative independence of the community of "common natures" from human thought, that one discovers the basic

---

[25] D6,S4,N6.   [26] See note 18, above.

difference between Scotus and Suarez. Both writers want to say that the essences found in things are in some sense *potentially* but not actually universal. Suarez's theory is that the form in the individual is *universalizable* because it can become a universal concept; but this, as he admits, is universality by analogy of attribution. While Scotus nowhere denies that the form in a particular thing is potentially universal in this sense, he holds a stronger view: that the form of a particular man is potentially or fundamentally universal in another sense, in the sense that it is intrinsically and of its very nature *communicable* (or, capable of being made common) to other particulars; the one and the same form can be shared by many particulars: when we say that several things have a common nature, we are saying that they have the same form; when we say several men are possible, we presuppose communicability. He argues that if the form of the individual were not of itself communicable to many, then, since to conceive it universally is to conceive it as communicable, the mind must necessarily distort reality in all its concepts. While Suarez concedes that "rationem universalitatis ut sic in duo consistere, scilicet in unitate et communicabilitate,"[27] he contends that both the unity and the communicability of the common nature are mind-dependent. "Haec ergo duo, scilicet unitas et communitas, explicanda sunt, ut constet, rationem constituentem proprium universale non reperiri in rebus, secluso intellectu."[28] But he denies that this is a falsification of reality; in fact, he argues that universality cannot exist apart from the intellect. His argument is essentially this: there can be only two kinds of unity: formal and numerical; and these two are distinguished by the mind, not by any real composition in things. To Scotus' claim that there is another kind of unity, the unity of the common nature, which is common to all individuals of a species, Suarez replies by denying the supposition of Scotus' opinion:[29] namely, that the specific nature is prior in order of nature to the individuals and, as a result, has its own "unity of precision," "unity of isolation," or "common numerical unity." If there is no point in saying that the nature is prior to the individual, then there is no sense in saying the nature has its own unity. So, Suarez argues that any claim that two things are so related that one is prior in order of nature to the other presupposes an additional claim that these two things are really related causally. But, he says, the specific nature in John and the individuality of John are not distinct apart from our way of conceiving them and, on the general principle that when there is no distinction *ex natura rei*, there cannot be a real order or real causality, it follows that there cannot be a priority of nature. The question is thus turned into the most fundamental

[27] D6,S2,N9.
[28] *Ibid.*

[29] D6,S3,N8.

point of disagreement between Suarez and Scotus: the nature of distinction *ex natura rei.*

Scotus declares that there is a distinction *a parte rei* between the formal and the individual unities in a particular thing, while Suarez denies this.[30] Exactly the same thing happens when Suarez argues that "the disposition of the common nature to be in many things is not something belonging to the nature itself, in so far as it exists *a parte rei.*"[31] For his main premise in his arguments is: (1) that the human nature in Peter is not disposed to be in anything else, but is rather *opposed* to being common: "nec fieri potest ut natura humana, verbi gratia, existens in Petro eadem secundum rem amittat individuationem quam habet in Petro, et aquirat aliam." This is the very point Scotus would dispute. Stated as Suarez has it, even Scotus must admit that the individual nature is not communicable; but Scotus never meant, in saying that the nature is communicable, that the nature in Peter might *loose* its individuation and take up another in John. The apparent absurdity is a consequence of Suarez' statement of Scotus' position, not in the latter's but in the former's terms. Scotus did not infer, just because he holds that the nature is *a parte rei* distinct from the individuality of the thing, that they must be separable. *That* inference follows from Suarez's premises, not Scotus'.

Suarez offers various arguments to show that there can be no communicability in the formal nature of anything (apart from the consideration of it by the mind); the most interesting is:

> a universal nature could not exist in many things unless it was identical in being with the singulars; but such a nature identical in being with one individual cannot, while being the same thing, be identified in reality and with a real existence, with other things. Therefore such a nature, as it is in reality communicated to individuals and as it exists in them, cannot have a real disposition to be in many things.[32]

Again the major premise of the argument is another version of the point contested: "Major certa est ex supra dictis, in quibus ostendimus *universale non distingui a singularibus ex natura rei*"; for as Suarez interprets it, it is impossible for the nature to be thus distinct from the singulars; but not so for Scotus. The nub of the disagreement is in the expression *ex natura rei.*

7) *Analysis of the Contested Distinction*—In order to be clear about what Suarez affirms and Scotus denies in this basic assumption from which so many things follow, one should consider the conditions re-

---

[30] D6,S1,N18 and D5,S2,N9, in extenso.   [32] D6,S4,N4.
[31] D6,S4,N2.

quired for a distinction *ex natura rei*.[33] A distinction *ex natura rei* is an *actual distinction, a parte rei,* not a distinction dependent upon the fact that the things in question have been differently conceived by the mind. The separability of the objective concepts of the things thought to be distinct (i.e., of the things-as-conceived) is a sufficient (Scotus denies that it is *necessary*) condition (generally) for an actual distinction *a parte rei.* The actual distinction *a parte rei* may be either a major real distinction or a distinction *ex natura rei,* which is also called by Suarez in his special terminology, a "modal distinction." While both the major real distinction and the modal distinction or distinction *ex natura rei* are independent of the mind, their conditions differ. For Suarez says that generally where the two things, said to be distinct, can be preserved apart from each other simultaneously and actually, there is a major real distinction; and also, if the two things are such that either one can be preserved immediately and by itself without the other and without any new assistance from a third thing, there is a major real distinction, e.g., the case of a statue holding a basketball.[34]

In this special sense, the common nature cannot be said to be really distinct from the individual which shares it, since upon our supposing that the individual is separated from the common nature, it follows that we must suppose the individual is lost; that is, the loss of one form is always followed by the acquisition of one or more new forms, and we would now have an individual of a different nature. Moreover, as Scotus himself says, if all the individuals be destroyed, there is no common nature.[35] But in this sense of "real distinction" neither Scotus nor his followers proposed that the common nature was distinct from the individual. Rather, they proposed that a formal distinction *a parte rei*[36] (Suarez did not consider this a distinction *ex natura rei,* although Scotus did), did obtain between the common nature and the individuals. Fonseca gave as one criterion of a distinction *a parte rei:* "when one thing produces and another is what is produced," where the mode of production is real, of course. Suarez, agreeing in principle, says:

---

[33] Suarez' theory of distinctions is explained at length in the Seventh Disputation: *On the Various Kinds of Distinctions,* Trans. of Cyril Vollert, S.J. (Milwaukee: Marquette University Press, 1947).

[34] Suarez says, D7,S2,N9: "A distinction is real if both extremes can be preserved apart actually and simultaneously from the real union between them." And, "A distinction is real if one extreme can be preserved immediately and by itself without the other and vice versa, to the exclusion of any ordination to or necessary connection with a third thing."

[35] VII *Met.,* q,13,n23 "Potest enim et universale corrumpi ab actu esse, corruptis omnibus singularitus." See also: *Rep.* II, d3,q1,n5; *Ox.* II, d3, q7,n.4.

[36] *Ox.*I,d2,q4,a5, 41-45; *Ox.*I,d8,q4,a3, 17; *Ox.*II,d3,q1.

Nevertheless, I think it is true without qualification that there is among created things a certain actual distinction which is found in nature prior to any activity of the mind and that such a distinction is not as great as the distinction between two altogether separate things or entities. This distinction, to be sure, could be designated by the general term "real," in as much as it is truly *a parte rei* and is not merely an extrinsic denomination of the intellect. However, to differentiate it from the other, namely the major real distinction, we can call it either a distinction *ex natura rei*, thus applying to this imperfect distinction a term which is in common use; or more properly, a "modal distinction."[37]

The "convincing argument" that a modal distinction (and not a major real distinction) obtains between two entities is the fact that one extreme can be removed without loss of the other, whereas the process cannot be reversed. The swiftness can be removed from the running, with the preservation of the running, but not vice versa.[38]

The formal distinction as conceived by Duns Scotus, however, is not a subdivision of the distinction Suarez calls modal.[39] It is totally different. For Scotus says the formal distinction holds between realities which are not *formally identical*, realities which are such that in order to get the one alone, one needs a formal cause different from that required to get the other alone; the realities are such that one is conceivable without the other; but in any given thing having both formalities, the realities or formalities are not separable even by the power of God. An example is: Animality and Rationality in man.[40]

To be faithful to the thought of Scotus one should make it explicit that one is considering "parts" of a given real individual, parts which are separately conceivable and which are thereby called "parts", but which cannot exist separately without the destruction of the entity originally supposed; and yet, these parts can be conceived *as if they were* the formal causes of separate things, and they are such that if they were formal causes of separate things, they would produce things

---

[37] D7,S1,N16.

[38] D7,S2,N6: "Separation of one thing from another, if the separation is merely non-mutual (as it is commonly called), that is, a separation in which one extreme can remain without the other, but not conversely, is a convincing argument for a modal distinction but not for a greater distinction, namely a real distinction in the technical sense."

[39] It is only because of the ambiguity of the word "formal" that it sometimes appears that the class of formal distinction has some direct relation to the class of modal distinctions (D7,S1,N16).

[40] Grawjewski formulates the distinction as follows: "Distinctio formalis est distinctio ex natura rei intercedens inter plures formalitates realiter identificatas, quarum una ante opus intellectus conceptibilis est sine alia, licet separatim existere non potest ne quidem potentia divina": *The Formal Distinction of Duns Scotus* (Washington: Catholic University Press, 1944), p. 93.

[21]

which would be, among themselves, essentially different. Such parts are not separable—such parts are not merely mind-dependent in their distinction; such a distinction is neither a major real nor a modal distinction. Hence, among real distinctions less than "major real," Scotus places the formal distinction in addition to the modal distinction and considers *both* to be distinctions *ex natura rei* even though separability is entirely excluded from formal distinction.

Now, if we reexamine Suarez's basic premise that[41] the fundamental universal (here taken to be the same as the common nature) is not distinguished from the singulars *ex natura rei*, we see that as Suarez defines a distinction *ex natura rei*, one could indeed not make sense in supposing that the common nature could be really separated from its singularity or particularity in an individual, without the concomitant destruction of both the individual and the common nature. Scotus grants this.[42] Yet, he supposes that there is a *formal* distinction *a parte rei* between the common nature and the individuating principle in the particular. And since things which are only formally distinct entirely exclude separability of *any* part, even by God, it follows that Suarez's arguments based upon the fact that the common nature cannot be separated from the individuals do not prove that these factors are not distinct *ex natura rei* (as Scotus would understand the term). Hence, Suarez's arguments do not establish, against Scotus, that both the unity and the communicability of the common nature must arise from the operations of the mind and must apply *only* to the objective *forms* or objective natures (the natures as-conceived-by-the-mind) and cannot apply to the forms or natures apart from the operations of the mind.

Matters of considerable importance in Suarez's argument are thus seen to turn upon the phrase "distinct *ex natura rei*" and it is of some moment that the phrase "distinct *ex natura rei*" does not have the same meaning for Suarez and Scotus, since the former did not think it included the *formal* distinction, while the latter did.

However one may assess the success of Suarez's arguments that the unity of the common nature is dependent upon the operation of the conceiving mind and is found in things only fundamentally, one can clearly see that he rejects the view attributed to Scotus: namely, that there is a common nature in things, prior to their consideration by the mind, and having a unity of its own which is sufficient for it to be designated a *universale in re*, albeit potentially, but still in a *literal* and not merely attributional sense.

Although both Suarez and Scotus accept the claim that: "the nature of the individual is potentially universal," they assign two entirely different meanings to it; Scotus takes it literally as ascribing a non-

[41] D6,S4,N4.   [42] See note 35, above.

denominative property to the nature; Suarez interprets it as involving an analogy of attribution with respect to the causal relation of individual and concept in the intellect. The same sort of difference of meaning occurs in their analyses of the statement: "Things which are similar share a form" and in other crucial assertions regarding "similarity," "communicability," and other characteristics of the *fundamentum in re.*

8) *The Genetic Psychology of Universal Concepts*—Although the main object of the disputation is the metaphysical doctrine already summarized, certain auxiliary psychological claims are made, claims which are more extensively developed in the posthumous *De Anima*. Since the psychological theory of St. Thomas is so well known, and since Suarez uses it in a continuing comparison, let us consider the respects in which Suarez departs from St. Thomas.

There are seven phases in Suarez's alteration of St. Thomas' position: (1) He says the impressed species produced by the agent intellect is not "abstract" in the sense of "universalized"; rather it is "abstract" in the sense of "dematerialized." The agent intellect performs *formal,* not universal or metaphysical abstractions. The process by which the form or structure which is realized in, for example, the architect's drawings and specifications of the Empire State Building, in the granite and steel building itself and in the plaster and plastic scale model, becomes an object of thought as a result of our examining these "embodiments" is *formal abstraction;* it is the process of coming to understand a formal-structure *apart from* any particular kind of material in which the form can be realized (although it is obvious that not every form can be realized is in *every* kind of material and equally obvious that some forms can be realized in many kinds of material). Dematerialization of a form, or formal abstraction, results in a mental sign which potentially at least has great generality. Aquinas wants to say it has this *actually* and immediately; Suarez and Scotus say it has it only potentially, that the mind must learn by comparing the species of things that the form is actually common, i.e., that it is actually found in many things and, perhaps, in many material kinds of things. (2) The intellectual impressed species produced by the agent intellect and received in the possible intellect is the intellectual species of a singular thing. (3) From this impressed species the possible intellect can either produce a formal concept of the singular or various formal concepts which are universal. (4) The universal concepts are derived by *comparison* by the possible intellect of the several species defined in different formal abstractions.[43] Hence, (5) the universal is not what is known first by the intellect; rather, it is the individual which is first

[43] IV *De An.*, Ch. 3, n.13.

[23]

known. (6) The two kinds of abstraction are essentially different; *formal abstraction* has nothing to do with universality, while *universal abstraction* is not an activity of the agent intellect. (7) The impressed species, not being universal, is not a formal similitude of the thing but is only a virtual likeness of the thing; it is called a "likeness" by analogy of attribution.

The difference between Aquinas and Suarez on the matter of abstraction must be traced to a difference on a more fundamental issue; namely, individuation. Aquinas holds that dematerialization implies universalization, since he does not admit a middle between particularity and universality, and since the individuation of a thing is derived from its materiality. This was also the view of Albert the Great. Suarez, on the other hand, holds that individuation is derived from the *form* and hence, counterargued that dematerialization has no such implication of universalization. Given St. Thomas' theory of individuation, a form separated from matter by the agent intellect is not individuated and becomes, by the mere fact of separation, universal. Since, for Suarez, the individuation is intrinsic to the form, such separation will not result in universalization; the form will remain the form of a particular, and it is only by the comparison and further abstraction of the possible intellect that the form is rendered universal. The other points of difference mentioned above follow from Suarez's position on the first.

As was remarked, the "universal abstraction" performed by the possible intellect is different from the formal abstraction of the agent intellect. The abstraction of universals is distinguished by three features: (1) the dematerialization by which the form is rendered potentially communicable—formal abstraction; (2) the formation of a concept which potentially contains many inferiors or singulars; (3) the formation of this concept by *comparison* of the impressions of particulars. Suarez says: "The intellect knows universals in a proper concept, by abstracting from singulars or not caring about them. This stands from experience, for we consider 'man' by not considering Peter and Paul."[44]

It will be noticed that there is nothing about Suarez's psychological doctrine which could warrant anyone's charging him with psychological idealism, since all the concepts formed by a finite mind clearly have individual things as causal determinants.

(9) *Was Suarez a Moderate Realist?*—Suarez subscribes to the moderate realist formula "*Universalitas est per intellectum cum funda-*

---

[44] IV *De An.*, Ch. 3, n.11: "Intellectus cognoscit proprio conceptu universalia, abstrahendo a singularibus, seu non curando de illis. Haec constat ex experientia, consideramus enim hominem non considerando Petrum et Paulum."

mento in re"[45] which has been traditionally (but, of course, quite un-foundedly) held to distinguish the moderate realist from the concep-tualists and nominalists. After one has examined this matter with care, one sees that the basic difference between the views of Suarez, Scotus, Occam, and Aquinas is not over whether the writers will accept this formula; for even Occam and his fourteenth century followers sub-scribe to it, as could most of the philosophers who have been called conceptualists. Rather, the basic differenec in views centers on whether and how the *fundamentum in re* has causal control over the formal concepts to be produced, and on the analysis of expressions of the form: "A and B are of the *same* nature"; "The same form is found in all men," etc. For a theory which holds that the conception of several in-dividuals via the same concept, and therefore the ascription of the same form to things is causally determined not by the particular indi-vidual, but by the intellect, will differ much more markedly from the particular-realism of Suarez than does the alledged common-nature-realism of Scotus.

The realism of Suarez consists entirely in the fact that *what* formal concept the possible intellect possesses and employs in considering a given singular or group of similar singulars in determined not by the mind alone, but is determined *formally* by the thing; the form in the particular thing becomes the formal cause of the content of the im-pressed species, and, derivatively, of the formal concept in the possible intellect.[46] Thus universal concepts, like the singular concepts (and for Suarez there are both), are not entirely products of the mind and the mind is not entirely free to form concepts for its own purposes; rather what concepts are formed is also a function of what things there are and what things are experienced, since the forms in things are the *fundamentum* or formal determinants of the concepts in the mind. This is all the moderate realism there is in Suarez.

I have said that Suarez is a *particular-realist* as opposed to a *com-mon-nature-realist* (like Scotus). By this I mean that Suarez held that there was a *real fundamentum in re* for our universal concepts to be found in *particular* things and that it is "universal" in just the same sense in which a stop light at which no one has ever looked may be red. This is realism of a very sophisticated sort.[47] Whether Suarez is

---

45 D6,S5,N1.
46 Such talk of "formal cause" is meta-phorical since, as Suarez says, quali-ties do not have forms in the way substances do.
47 However, in making this strong claim that Suarez is a realist, I do not pre-tend that all the difficulties in Suarez's views have been explained, vindicated or even stated. That mat-ter will be treated elsewhere. But I do mean that mere similarity be-tween Occam and Suarez, or even his substantial agreement with Peter Aureoli, does nothing to advance the charge of nominalism.

properly classified as a "moderate-realist" will depend on other considerations than his acceptance of the general formula. Since these points cannot be developed here, let us leave the question open, but with the reminder that there is no evidence whatever for calling Suarez a nominalist.

The unity of the scholastic tradition on universals is illustrated by a list of metaphysical points on which Aquinas, Scotus, Occam, and Suarez all agree and an indication of the one or two major points on which there is substantial disharmony, although there existed a common tradition as to mode of discussion.

All four authors are agreed that: (1) There are no universals to be found existing independently both of the operations of the mind and of the existence of singular things; and further that such a notion is inconsistent. (2) Anything that really *exists* (that is, exists independently of consideration by the human mind and of any mind other than the Divine Mind) is a particular or singular thing, a primary substance. (3) Whatever is actually universal is an *ens rationis,* a mental being called a "concept," whose existence (analogically speaking) is derived from the operations of the conceiving mind. (4) There is a *foundation in re* and independently of the operations of the mind for the universality of the concept which is actually universal. (5) The foundation *in re* is, at least in part, the *form* found in the individual. (6) The foundation *in re* can be called a *universal* by extrinsic denomination, i.e., by analogy of attribution based upon the causal relation which holds between the foundation *in re* and the actual universal found in the mind.[48] (7) The universal concept is formed by the mind through a process called "abstraction"; (on this point there are many important distinctions and differences which will not be treated herein). (8) There is a real similarity in things of the same nature, a similarity which is the foundation of the "commonness" of the nature or quiddity.

Other than differences in psychology which we must gloss over, the chief discrepancies among these authors are found in the following areas: (1) the manner in which the forms in individuals are the foundation *in re* for the universal concept and (2) the analysis of the claim that two things are similar because they have something in common. There are several notions of commonness or community involved, sev-

---

[48] At first sight it might appear that Occam would deny this; but his statement that nothing extra-mental is to be called universal, clearly had in mind literal or proper predication. He had no interest in analogous talk and might still have resisted the point; but his own position compels acquiescence, since he holds for causal dependence of concepts upon particular things. Scotus, too, might seem to resist; but by the same arguments would have to agree, since his position is stronger and entails this one.

eral interpretations of the expression "common nature" and consequently several analyses of the expression "the form in the individual is the foundation *in re* for the universality of the concept." These two points are intimately connected, since for each of the four authors, and especially for Suarez, the explanation of the similarity of things is directly connected with the explanation of the foundation of universality.

In brief, Suarez and Scotus are very similar in their psychological doctrine of universals, whereas Aquinas, Occam, and Suarez are all much closer together on the metaphysics of the matter than any one of them is to Scotus, who stands closer to Plato and Augustine. Suarez's view is truly a syntheses of the work of his predecessors, and comparison with those writers should not be used to make him join some older "camp," but should function merely to clarify the various strands of tradition woven into his original design.[49]

Finally a comparison of starting points is useful:

1) Scotus says we must postulate community (which is a logical consequence of possibility) of natures and must seek causal explanations of universality and singularity, which are logically posterior to community.

2) Occam says we must postulate singularity as a principle of explanation, not itself explicable, and proceed to explain universality and community, which are logically posterior.

3) Suarez and Aquinas say we must have a principle of individuation to explain singularity and must also seek explanations of community and universality, which are logically posterior to the principles of composition (essence-existence, matter-form) through which we solve the problem of the one and the many. As a result, all three factors, universality, communicability, and individuation must be explained in terms of prior metaphysical principles.

[49] The richness of Suarez's *Disputation on Universals* cannot be tapped in an introduction. A much more extensive analysis of Suarez's theory will be forthcoming from the author in a general history of the discussion of universals during the middle ages.

Note to the Reader

1. The divisions of the text, other than Section titles, are not always placed on the page in the same way as they occur in the Latin text from which we translated, though otherwise they are unaltered. In the translator's opinion the leading phrases which subdivide the text do not come from Suarez's pen.

2. Double quotation marks fulfill a variety of important functions throughout this translation. They mark off phrases or statements which are actually quoted from other writers or locations; they indicate phrases which appear in a new or unusual meaning, especially phrases which are coined or created through hyphenating words; they surround phrases which supposit materially, and most importantly of all, those which supposit simply (stand for what is *signified* by the term rather than for what is denoted). The use of expressions such as "man," "horse," "accident," "property," and "universal" in simple supposition is dialectically crucial to the arguments of: Section II, n.12; Section IV, n.4 and n.6; throughout Section VIII; Section IX, n.4, 9, 15, 25, and 26; and throughout Section X. The reader should keep clearly in mind that a phrase may stand for its own meaning alone and not for any individual at all.

3. Again conjecturing that the morass of semi-colons we find in the Latin text did not originate with Suarez, we have occasionally altered the punctuation by substituting periods. On a few occasions we have dropped particles and incidental words which are repeated endlessly. There are also occasional alterations in strict translation of the grammar; but these are few indeed.

4. We have also on aesthetic but not logical grounds accorded with a convention which allows quotation marks to "capture" periods and commas which would otherwise immediately follow and which govern expressions of which the quoted phrase is only a part. Since quotation marks were not part of Suarez's text, where we sometimes find the genitive case as a substitute, there is no violation of the original in such a concession to technology.

Francis Suarez

ON FORMAL AND UNIVERSAL UNITY

Disput VI

After individual or numerical unity, we must consider formal, and consequently, universal unity, which is in a way opposed to numerical unity; for numerical unity involves incommunicability with respect to inferiors, whereas formal and universal unity intrinsically requires a nature communicable to many inferiors. We must especially consider whether the formal and universal unities are in any way real, whether they are separate unities or whether they in any way coalesce. Similarly, we must consider how many kinds of each there may be, and what the principle in things might be which accounts for each; and, finally, how and through which operation of the understanding each is arrived at.

Section I

Whether There May Be In Real Things Some Formal Unity Distinct from and Less than Numerical Unity

1. *There is reason for doubt on both sides.* The reason for doubting is that since it has been said in the preceding disputation[1] that all things which are in the world are individuals, it is thus repugnant that there should be among real things some true being which is not both individual and singular; neither can it be, therefore, that there should be in reality some true and real unity besides numerical or individual unity. There is doubt on the other hand, however, since "the one" is nothing else than "individual being," as Aristotle said, 4 *Metaphysics*, text 3, and Book 10, text 2; but besides the individual numerical undividedness, which is called "material," there is found in things an essential or formal undividedness by which several men, for example, although materially or in number distinct, are nevertheless of the same essence and nature; therefore, besides numerical unity, formal unity is to be found in reality.

On What the Writers Agree or Disagree About

2. On this matter the Thomists and Scotists agree, teaching that a formal unity, in some way distinct from numerical unity, is to be found

---

[1] *Disputation V: On Individual Unity,* Vol. 24, pp. 145-201, passim; F. Suarez, *Opera* Omnia, ed. by A. Carolo Berton, (Paris: Vives, (1856-66).

in real things. Thus Scotus, in 2, dist 3, q.1; and 7 *Metaph.* quaest 10; and in the same place, Anthony Andreas, quaest 17; and Cajetan, *De Ente est Essentia,* c.4, q.6; and Soncinas, 7 *Metaphysics,* q.4, says that the nature considered in itself, that is, as it prescinds from the being it has in individuals or through the intellect, has some unity; and Javellus book 8, *Metaphysics,* question 13 holds the same opinion; moreover, St. Thomas is found to teach this opinion explicitly in the *Opusculum de Natura Generis,* Ch. 7; this could not be true except of formal unity, since it could not be true of individual unity, because "nature" thus taken is said to prescind from the being of individuals. But the aforementioned authors disagree in the manner of explaining this formal unity; however, the difference seems to consist chiefly in two things. First, in this, that Scotus thinks this formal unity, or the nature itself as formally one, is formally and *ex natura rei*[2] distinct from the individual unity or difference. Others think they are distinct only by a distinction of reason; whose opinion seems better proved to us was explained in Section 2 of the preceding disputation[3] and will be touched upon again in following sections.

Secondly, they differ in that Scotus does not think this formal unity or the nature considered as having this formal unity, is multiplied in number in the individuals themselves, but that all the individuals of the same nature have one and the same formal unity, one (I say), not only mentally but really; or that the nature insofar as it really exists in many individuals, has only one formal unity. Others think the nature in single individuals has a formal unity mentally distinct from numerical unity, and that this is truly multiplied in individuals along with the individual unities, and consequently that there is not some unity which is the same in many individuals through a truly real unity, but that such unity exists merely through some kind of agreement or similarity. And on this point also, the latter opinion is more probable, although

[2] The expression *"ex natura rei,"* which occurs with great frequency and in places of great importance in the disputation wil not be translated, since the various grammatical contexts in which it occurs would require such widely differing forms of translation that the reader would in all probability often not realize that a highly technical point had been made. Instead the reader is hereby informed that a *distinction ex natura rei* is, for Suarez, a special kind of real distinction, obtaining in reality independently of any consideration of things by any mind, between things only one of which can be separated and preserved apart from from the others. Discussion of the relationship of this distinction to the formal distinction (so often invoked by Duns Scotus) is to be found in the introduction to this translation, pages 19-23. Suarez, himself describes this distinction in *Disputation VII,* Section 1, number 16. A translation of this *Disputation On the Various Kinds of Distinctions,* by Cyril Vollert, S.J., is published by Marquette University Press, 1947.

[3] *Disputation V: On Individual Unity.*

some people think the difference is only in the manner of speaking; for what the Thomists call a "mental distinction," Scotus and others call a "formal distinction"; and what the Thomists call "agreement" or "similarity," Scotus calls "unity"; but whatever may be the intention of this or that author, we have not sufficiently explained what may be the distinction *ex natura rei* which we deny intervenes between the individual and the common essence; for we deny every distinction which could obtain in reality in any manner whatever, prior to the functioning of the mind. But we have also to speak, in the same sense and with the correlative concept, about the unity which is opposed to distinction, when we ask whether the nature, either in itself or in the particular thing, isolated from every act of understanding, has such a formal unity, (which is true and real unity) that it may have it entirely of itself and retain it in all the individuals.

THE BASIS OF THE EARLIER OPINION

3. *First.* In order that the truth be better explained, the opinion of Scotus must be urged somewhat. First, Aristotle, 5 *Metaphysics*, text 8 and 12, placed unity of species and genus among the kinds of "one," since in some way these unities are real; for here there was no discussion of intentions of reason, but only of the unity which is a characteristic [passion] of being, and which must be in some way real; the unity of genus and species can best be real on account of the formal unity. Whence in 7 *Metaphysics*, text 51, Aristotle says the same thing: that the nature "animal" is the same in all the species; and in 2 *De Anima*, text 88, he says that the nature "transparency" is the same in air and water.

4. *Secondly.* A second reason is taken from St. Thomas, above, that the human nature which exists in Peter and Paul can be defined by a unique and proper definition, as is self-evident; therefore, as such it has some unity; but it does not have that unity through the agency of the mind; therefore it has it of itself; therefore it is a true and real unity. The first inference stands, since nothing can be defined except insofar as it is one, witness Aristotle, 4 *Metaphysics*, text 10, and 7 *Metaphysics*, text 13. The minor premise is proved by the fact that a nature does not derive its definability from the intellect but from itself; therefore, neither does it get that unity which is necessary for a definition from the intellect. Everything, however, which accrues to a nature, but not through the agency of the intellect, is real and either positive or by way of a privation which is sufficient for unity (which formally consists in privation).

5. *Thirdly.* An objection is dissolved—Whence I argue, thirdly, that unity consists in undividedness; but human nature of itself has formal

[31]

undividedness; therefore of itself it has formal unity. The minor is clear, since human nature of itself has no formal division; because if it had it of itself, it would have it everywhere and always, and could not be conceived without it; but human nature is perfectly conceived without such division; therefore of itself it has no such division; thus it is of itself undivided since undividedness is nothing but the lack of division. That the nature is of itself negatively one and undivided since it does not of itself have that which is divided and many, but is nevertheless not positively one and undivided (as the Thomists are often given to saying), does not seem to be satisfactory. For it seems that an absurdity is involved in this distinction; since nothing is positively one, but only negatively; nor can undividedness as such accrue to anything except through the negation of division; therefore, if the nature has of itself this negation of division, then of itself it has the undividedness and therefore the unity which consists in the undividedness. And this is both confirmed and emphasized; for, if the nature has of itself the negation of division, then division will be incompatible with it, because that which belongs to a nature from itself is inseparable from it, and its contradictory is thereby rendered always incompatible; therefore the lack of division intrinsically belongs to it and consequently positively belongs insofar as it can belong by reason of its foundation. It may perhaps be said that neither division nor formal undividedness belongs to the nature of itself, but that the nature is in some way indifferent to both, just as a surface is of itself neither white nor non-white but only negatively can be said not to be white. In that sense, it seems, we must take the common reply that undividedness or the negation of division does not belong to a nature of itself positively, but only negatively; for these terms [positively and negatively] do not refer to "undividedness," but to this, namely, "to belong of itself," so that the meaning may be that a nature does not of itself involve division, for neither does it of itself involve the lack of division or unity. In this sense, sometimes negation can rightly belong to something of itself positively, and sometimes negatively; for lack of rationality belongs to an animal as such, negatively from the nature itself; to a beast, however, it belongs positively because it so accrues to it that the positive opposite form is incompatible with it. But I stand opposed to this; for even in this sense the nature seems to be positively formally undivided of itself since it so obtains the negation of division from itself, that all formal division is entirely incompatible with it; for although the nature may be materially divided in the individuals, nevertheless it cannot be formally divided since formal division is not different from essential division; "man," however, for example, cannot be

[32]

essentially divided even though "man" can be materially divided into many individuals.

6. Whence I argue *fourthly,* that human nature, e.g., of itself and positively is a being; therefore of itself and positively (in the sense expressed) it has a certain unity; and it is not material or individual, as was just shown above and is obvious in itself, since otherwise it could not be multiplied in number nor could it even be conceived without numerical unity; therefore the unity is merely formal, since it is not possible to think of any other which is midway between the two. The antecedent of the first premise is evident, since "being" belongs intrinsically and essentially not only to singular things but also to natures which are universally conceived by us. For these natures are not nothing entirely, nor of themselves are they several individual entities since the natures do not include the singular characteristics or the principles of individuation, but only the essential principles; therefore, each nature of itself is neither many things nor absolutely nothing, but is a real being and consequently one thing in some way, since some unity accrues to every being. This is confirmed, as human nature and the nature of horses, of themselves and apart from all individuating principles, are several and are really and essentially distinct; therefore, each of them is of itself formally and essentially one, for a plurality supposes unities and division from others supposes undividedness in the thing itself.

7. So from these latter points it can be concluded that this formal unity is common to all individual things in which the nature which is said to be formally one, is common; it is not possible that the nature be common unless its unity be common. Again, since this formal unity has nothing by which it could be divided into several unities, (a) it would either be divided into several formal unities; and this cannot be, since by its very notion it must be formally undivided and in this consists its unity; or (b) it is divided into several material and individual unities; and thus the formal unity as such is not divided but is communicated to many, which is what we intend. Finally, since otherwise the formal and individual unity could not be distinguished in the individuals themselves, in what way would they be different if both were to be multiplied? For whatever is multiplied in this way is an individual.

THE TRUE OPINION IS CONFIRMED

8. In order for us to explain the contrary and true opinion, we must first remark that there is given in real things a formal unity *per se* belonging to each essence or nature. On this, everyone agrees, and the arguments in favor of Scotus prove this. Also, since "unity" means "lack of division," there are as many kinds of unity as there are kinds of

[33]

divisions; but in things there is a material and a formal, or an entitiative and an essential division; therefore, there is similarly a formal unity besides the material unity. As a result, any individual, for example, Peter, is not only one in number, but is also one essentially; and the individual has both unities in reality and not as a result of the operations of the mind; for just as numerical division is lacking on the part of the thing, so also, there is lacking essential division, whether specific or generic; since formal unity is nothing other than essential unity, it follows . . . [that there is a formal unity in each individual].

9. *Formal unity is distinguished from singular unity by the mind.* Secondly it must be remarked that this formal unity is distinguished at least by reason from individual unity. This is proved by the argument put forward in behalf of Scotus. And this is quickly rendered obvious, since the common nature is in some way, at least by reason, distinct from individuals, and as thus distinct it does not have individual unity, although it retains formal unity; those unities therefore differ at least in concept. Similarly, individual unity does not belong to the common essence by itself, but it is necessary to understand that something, distinct at least in concept, has been added, by which that common essence is made individual; formal unity, however, of itself immediately belongs to that common essence without anything's being contributed even through reason. Nevertheless, although one can prescind from the individual unity, it is not possible to conceive the essence unless this formal unity from which one cannot entirely prescind, accompany it; therefore these two unities are distinct by reason, in the same way in which in an individual thing the essence, as essence, and the entity (as such an individual and singular thing) are distinguished.

10. *It is not distinguished "ex natura rei."* Whence I say thirdly; these unities are not distinguished on the part of the thing or *ex natura rei.*[4] This conclusion follows from what was said in the preceding disputation. And it is proved: since the common essence and the singular entity are not distinguished *ex natura rei,* but by reason alone; therefore, formal and individual unities cannot be distinguished *ex natura rei* but only by reason. Besides, the nature itself, could it be considered by us in itself (that is, according to those characteristics which belong to it of itself as it is isolated in the mind from individuals), is nevertheless not truly a real being, unless it is in individuals; for "when first substances are destroyed, it is impossible that anything remain," as Aristotle said in the chapter *On Substance;* and nothing can have real existence apart from individuals and without which [existence] nothing can truly be a real being, either in act or in potency, as was said

[4] See note 2, above, and pp. 19-23 of Introduction.

above concerning "being." Therefore, the nature in itself does not have reality except in individuals; so, neither can there be true and real unity unless in individuals; thus, there can be no formal unity in the thing itself which would be distinct *ex natura rei*, from the singular unity of each individual. This last inference is clear from the fact that whatever is intrinsic in an individual thing and is essential to it is not distinguished from it *ex natura rei*.

11. *Formal unity, as it exists in a thing, is incommunicable.* From these things it is concluded fourthly that this formal unity, insofar as it exists in things prior to any operation of the understanding, is not common to many individuals, but that formal unities are multiplied as many times as there are individuals. This is proved, first, since this formal unity accompanies the nature on account of itself; but in a real thing there is not any *common* nature; but the nature and essence are multiplied as many times as there are individuals, as is obvious from what was said above and what we shall say again in what follows: therefore, the same must be said of formal unity which is, as it were, an intrinsic and transcendental property of such a nature; and as a result they follow one another and, the one being multiplied, the other is also, according to the teaching of Aristotle in 4 *Metaphysics*, text 3. Secondly, formal unity as it exists on the part of a thing, is not distinguished *ex natura rei* from individual unity, as has been said; therefore it must be multiplied in the thing itself when the individuals and their individual unities are multiplied; therefore there is no formal unity in reality, common to many things of the same kind. The first inference is proved, since, if formal and individual unity be not distinguished *ex natura rei*, then in a given individual, Peter, for instance, formal unity and his individual unity are not distingushed; therefore they are distinguished from the formal and individual unity of Paul; since, by this very fact that the formal unity of Peter is in fact entirely the same as his individual unity, it is necessary that it be distinguished from the individual unity of Paul, because it is impossible for something to be identical with an entirely distinct and somewhat opposed thing. Thirdly, whatever exists on the part of the thing is singular, and consequently incommunicable, or not common to several inferiors, as was shown in section 1 of the preceding disputation and will be also stated in the following section; but this unity is real and exists in its own way on the part of the thing, as has been shown; therefore it is singular; therefore it is not common in reality. The last inference is clear, since what is singular is proper to some individual and thus cannot be common to many things, and because of that, such community requires abstraction from all individuals—something which cannot belong to things really, but only through the intellect.

[35]

12. And it follows from these things, first, that although some individual may be, on the part of the thing, formally one, apart from the thinking of the mind, nevertheless, several individuals which are said to be of the same nature are not one thing with true unity which is "found in" the things, but are one thing only fundamentally or through the intellect. But for this reason Aristotle sometimes, when he says several things are one in essence or in formal notion, explains this unity through its relation to the understanding; that is, that they are conceived under one notion or definition, as is clear in 5 *Metaphysics,* Ch. 6, text 11, and book 10, at the beginning. And St. Thomas, in *De Ente et Essentia,* Ch. 4, says in effect, that the nature does not of itself have common unity, since otherwise it could not become singular. It follows secondly, that it is one thing to speak of formal unity and another to speak of the community of this unity, for unity is in things, as has been insisted; community, however, properly and strictly is not in things, because no unity which is found in reality is common, as we have shown, but there is in singular things a certain similarity in their formal unities on which the community which the intellect can attribute to such a nature as it is conceived, is based; which similarity is not properly unity, since it does not represent the undividedness of the entities on which it is based but only their congruence or relation or their co-existence.

The Bases of the Preceding Opinion Are Dissolved

13. To the first basis of the earlier opinion, it is answered that Aristotle included among the kinds of "one" generic and specific unity, either because of the formal unity which they bespeak in the single things in which they exist, or because they are in some way fundamentally in things, as we shall insist hereafter; and, in this way, several things are said to be of the same nature either by their identity in notion or by the fundamental unity which consists in similarity. Whence it is said to the second point, that this unity is sufficient in order that a nature may be defined, since the definition is not properly in the things, but in the concept; and thus, one definition is not common except insofar as the mind conceives something as common, by separating it from everything singular. For this, the formal unity, which the nature has in any individual whatever along with the similarity of all such unities among themselves is enough; for it arises from this that the intellect conceives and defines that formal notion in one common concept. Whence, when it is said that a nature does not have its definability through the agency of the intellect, it must be said that this is true fundamentally and remotely but not, however, true proximately, or

---

[5]*Disputation V: On Individual Unity.*

(what is the same) that it is true with regard to the essence which is explained in the definition, for the essence precedes in the thing but not indeed with respect to that condition, namely, community which the nature demands in order for us to define it; for this is had solely through the thinking of the mind.

14. With regard to the third point, it is said first to lead to the conclusion that the nature of itself has formal unity, but not community of this formal unity. Whence, it has an entirely inseparable unity, yet no community whatever; for in singular individuals the nature is formally one, it is not, however, common, nor is it indifferent to many things, but in each is singular, and its proper effect. Concerning this when one says that the nature of itself is formally undivided in such a way that it is repugnant for it to be formally divided, the meaning can be equivocal. For *either* the meaning is that the nature, which is formally one, is not further divisible by formal and essential differences; and in this sense, the statement is simply false with regard to the generic nature; for the generic nature has its formal unity, and yet it is nonetheless formally divisible through specific differences. In specific natures, however, it is indeed true, yet that has no relevance to the matter with which we are concerned; for although the specific nature may not be further divisible through essential divisions, it is nevertheless divisible through individual differences, and in each individual it has its formal unity, distinct from that which it has in others; and this suffices that such unity cannot be common in reality. *Or,* the meaning is that the nature is of itself so undivided that all division or multiplication of its formal unity is repugnant to it; and in this sense the assumption is simply false, even for specific natures. Since, as we were saying above, although there may not be division or essential distinction in individuals, there is, nevertheless, division or distinction of essences, so it must be said in the present instance that, although individuals of the same species are simply not said to differ formally, they nevertheless have distinct abstract formal unities proper to the singulars. For to be distinguished essentially or formally not only implies having a distinct essence or form, but also having dissimilarity and disharmony in essence, and also, what is more, implies being distinguished not only as things, but also with regard to the common notion and definition which the mind can make. To have a distinct essence or formal unity only implies an entitative and real distinction, in the way in which, just as Peter has a distinct humanity from Paul, he has also a distinct essence and distinct formal unity although they are similar in these things. To a nature therefore, which of itself is said to be formally one, it is not repugnant with regard to that formal unity that the nature be multiplied in many things and have that unity incommunicable in singulars,

[37]

and consequently be distinct from others; but dissimilarity or disharmony with regard to that aspect is alone repugnant, that is, that those things which share that formal unity should not be alike in it and agree among themselves.

15. The reply to the fourth point along with its confirmation is the same; for it proves that the common nature has of itself a formal unity regarding which, one specific nature differs from another formally and specifically; it does not prove, however, that the formal unity is common in reality itself, unless with respect to similarity or harmony, as has been insisted. And in almost the same way it is replied to the arguments by which it is proved finally, that this formal unity may be common in reality; for it is common just exactly as the nature itself of which it is the unity. The nature is not common with respect to a reality, but with respect to a notion or basic similarity, as has often been touched upon, and is taught in the following section. Therefore, the formal unity is common in the same way, the formal unity which is in reality divided into several formal unities each of which is formally undivided in itself; among themselves or one from another, they are not in fact formally undivided, unless with regard to the similarity or harmony, by reason of which they are not simply and properly said to be formally distinct, as has been said, but are formal unities entitatively or individually distinct. These two things do not conflict, namely, that formal unities themselves should be multiplied, and yet not be multiplied formally but materially, or in the individual; for that formal unity is also singular and individual in each indivdual, although it does not have that status by virtue of the formal unity but from the individual difference. We confess, therefore, that any formal unity insofar as it is in reality is individual and singular, but that it differs nonetheless in notion from individual unity, since formal unity of itself and from its proper concept expresses undividedness in the aforementioned essential notes; individual unity expresses undividedness in the entity itself. Whence, formal unity implies in the thing a basis of similarity with another thing of the same nature; individual unity, however, implies absolutely and simply a basis of distinction; and finally formal unity implies a basis of communicability at least with respect to concept; individual unity, however, implies entire incommunicability, in reality as well as in concept.

Section II

Whether the Unity of the Universal Nature Be Distinct from Formal Unity Actually in Reality, Prior to the Operation of the Mind

1. *Things which are denominated universals truly exist in reality.* First it must be established that those natures which we denominate[6] universal and common, are real and exist in things themselves; for we do not fabricate them mentally, but we rather apprehend them and understand them to be in things, and we produce definitions, construct demonstrations, and we seek knowledge of them as thus conceived. Thus Aristotle in 1 *Metaphysics,* Ch. 6, and Book 4, Ch. 5, rebukes Heraclitus and Cratylus because they said that there is in reality nothing besides singulars. And in 7 *Metaphysics,* text 56, he teaches that universals are not separate from things; and in texts 37 and 53 he says definitions are given of universal things, and in I *Post. Anal.,* texts 5, 11, 33, 39, and 43, he says that knowledge is of the universals which exist in singulars and which are abstracted from them; and he holds the same view in 1 *Metaphysics,* Ch. 1. And in the same sense, in I *De Interpretatione,* Ch. 5, he says that some things are universals, other singulars. And on this, all the philosophers and interpreters of Aristotle agree, with the exception of the nominalists who say terms are universal only in signifying, and concepts are universal only in representing, and definitions and knowledge are concerned proximately with these, as you can read in Occam I, dist 2, q.4, and *Quodlibet.* 5, questions 12 and 13; and Gabriol, in I, dist 7, 97 and 8; both of whom Fonseca has attacked extensively in Book 5, Ch. 28, q.2. And they are deservedly rebuked with regard to some ways of speaking; for perhaps in fact they do not disagree with the true view, for their reasons tend only to this, that they prove that universality is not in things but accrues to things insofar as they are objectively in the intellect, or accrues to things through denomination from some operation of understanding —which is true, as I shall say below. And indeed there is no need for us to be referring to and analyzing their arguments; for they in no way whatever prohibit its being true that the natures which are denominated universals should be in singulars and that the singulars themselves should have among themselves something in which they agree or are alike and something in which they differ or are distinguished. Whence, they falsely deny that demonstrations and definitions are given about

---

[6] "Denominate" is a technical expression, applied to the general class of "referrings," of which *intrinsic* and *extrinsic* denomination are the sub-classes. For an explanation of this term as it occurs in this text, see the Introduction, pages 8-10.

[39]

things, since sciences are not concerned with names or our formal concepts, but directly with things or objective concepts. For this reason, granted that the denomination of universality may accrue to things from concepts, nevertheless the things thus denominated are real and exist in reality.

2. *The universals in reality are not separate from the singulars.*— Secondly, it must be supposed that these things or natures which we denominate universals, are not really separated from singular things; since, as has been demonstrated above,[7] every thing which exists is necessarily singular and individual; and it clearly involves an absurdity that a man should exist, for instance, really separated from all singular men, and that he be universal with respect to all of them. For, if he is separate, he is not in them intrinsically and essentially; if, however, he is universal, he ought to be in them intrinsically and essentially since this is part of the notion of such a universal; nor indeed can he be simultaneously separated from them and intrinsically in them, since these two involve an absurdity when assumed to hold in the same reality.

Again, "man," as such, is either a thing distinct from Peter, Paul, etc., or "man," as such, is not a distinct thing; if the second of these is what is said, it is what we intend; for in this sense universals are said not to be separate since they are not things really distinct from singulars, and they do not have a proper entitative and real unity distinct from singulars; if the first be said, it would clearly follow that "man," as such, is some thing distinct from Peter and Paul, for a real distinction cannot be understood except between certain and determinate things; that thing would therefore be a certain man distinct from other men. Whence he could neither be of their essence nor could he be simultaneously in all of them. Again, one would be answered with the same reason that an animal separated from all species of animals, and a living being separated from all genera of living things, and thus of the other quidditative predicates—all of which are impossible, and useless besides, since it is required neither for knowledge nor for the production of definitions that we conjure ideal monsters of this kind.

3. *In what sense Plato claimed universals to be separated.* It is just as obvious and as self-evident as it seems incredible to many that Plato taught the contrary, in that sense in which in book 1 and 7 of the *Metaphysics* and in other places, Aristotle attributed it to him and extensively attacked it. St. Thomas refers to Eustratius' and Simplicius' having thought thus, in book 4 of *De Regimine Principum*, Ch. 4; and in particular, Augustine, treating of ideas in book 83, question 46,[8] and

---

[7] *Disputation V: On Individual Unity,* passim.

[8] It is not clear which passage of Augustine the author intends to refer to here.

in book 7, *De Civitate Dei*, Ch. 28, claims that Plato was talking about ideas which are in the divine mind, something which Seneca also thought, Book 8, Letter 66. Moreover, from Plato himself, in the *Parmenides* and the *Timaeus*, it seems to be indicated. It is to be read in Eugub., Book 1 *De Peren. Phil.*, Ch. 10. If this is so, Plato should consequently not be said to have posited ideas after our manner of conceiving, defining or understanding things in general; for ideas as they are in the mind of God contribute nothing to that, since we neither conceive nor define them; and if, *per impossibile*, there were no such ideas, universals could be conceived and defined by us in the same way. But ideas of that kind are posited in order to be the first exemplars of these inferiors, and they influence them as the first and immutable principle in its kind; there is a treatment of these ideas under this aspect by the Theologian in I, d.36, in St. Thomas, *Ia*, q. 15, and below we touch on the matter in treating of causes.[9] But whatever may be the mind of Plato, this consideration has no connection with the present matter since we are not concerned with the universal, which they call "in causing" whether it be by way of efficient or by way of exemplar cause, but with the universal-in-being, or in-predication.

THE MEANING OF THE QUESTION AND VARIOUS OPINIONS

4. Having supposed these things, the question is paramount whether a nature, which is denominated universal, although it may be in singular things, nonetheless has of itself sufficient unity (on account of which it can be called universal) so that not only the universal nature, but also its universality is in things. On this matter there are three opinions. The first is, that the nature has of itself and through itself some universality, so that even really existing in individuals themselves, it retains it and is universal in act: an opinion which John Monlorius defended in a special disputation on this matter, Ch. 5 and 6, and which is commonly attributed to Scotus in 2, d.3, q.1, and 7 *Metaphysics*, q. 18, where Anthony Andreas, q. 16 defends it. However, Scotus in the aforementioned distinction rather so talks that he simply denies that the universal is in act in things, and seems to admit only the universal in aptitude or potency—which Aristotle and everyone else concedes. For this reason, Scotus' disciples are at variance in explaining his opinion, as Fonseca, cited below, treated the matter extensively when he, like others, was trying to construe him according to his own opinion. But lest we should labor in equivocation we must clarify those terms "universal-in-act" and "universal-in-potency."

5. And so, if by "universal-in-act" one understands a nature abstracted from every individuation, and which is conceived in the man-

---

[9] Cf: *Disputation XXV: On Exemplary Cause*, Section I, number 3 and following.

ner of one disposition to be predicated of them, then it is self-evident that the "universal-in-act" as such is not in reality; and in this manner, Scotus explained this universality, above, and Aristotle talks in the same way when he denies in opposition to Plato that the universal is found in things, namely, subsisting universally and separate from every singular and individual contraction. Therefore, this universal is found only through the intellect, as we shall insist in the following section. Again, if by "universal-in-potency" one means, whatever does not have actual universality explained in the mentioned manner, but does, however, furnish a basis to the intellect for its conceiving or imagining it, it is thus also certain that the "universal-in-potency" *is* found in reality, since some basis is given in things for the abstraction or universal conception, which the intellect produces. But of what kind is this basis? For in this is the point of controversy. The opinion mentioned affirms that this basis is some universality, which of itself and really belongs to the nature, as it is prior in nature to its inferiors which contract it. For, granted that in reality the nature is not separated from them, nevertheless it is indeed common to all with respect to the same notion and formal unity. And thus this universality, although with regard to the former it is called dispositional or fundamental, nevertheless, with regard to the singularity or the individuation of the nature is true real and actual universality which differs from formal unity only in this: that it expresses, in addition to the negation of division in itself, indifference and community with regard to many things.

6. Therefore, the stated opinion is thus proved; first, because a nature, for instance, human nature, has formal unity of itself, as has been said; the fact that it is communicable to many, it also has of itself; therefore, of itself and prior to every intellect it is one "in many and of many," in which the notion universality consists, as Aristotle writes, *Post,* text 25; therefore the nature has of itself and in the things themselves some universality, which is its real property, and not merely of reason. The minor on which the strength of the argument rests, is proved first because human nature of itself is not incommunicable, otherwise it could not be numerically multiplied; therefore it is communicable of itself; between the communicable and the incommunicable no medium is found with respect to the same nature, for they are contradictory opposites. Secondly, the nature is not of itself "this" and individual, as has been proved in the preceding disputation, but requires some adjunct by which it is individuated; therefore of itself it is disposed to be contracted through individuating principles; indeed, because it is not disposed to subsist abstractly and universally, it posits and requires this determination to be able to subsist; it is therefore of itself disposed to that determination; therefore it is of itself communi-

[42]

cable to many individuals. This last inference is proved because such a nature is not adequately contractible through one individual difference alone—indeed this is repugnant to it; therefore, this repugnance, which such a nature has to being contracted to one single individual, is based upon the natural disposition which it has to being able to be in many things; this disposition therefore really belongs to it of itself. The same thing is proved, thirdly, from the characteristics of universal natures in as much as they are universal; for they are said to be the proper objects of the sciences, unchangeable and perpetual, ungenerable and incorruptible; they are also said to be the things immediately signified by the terms, or common concepts, among which the essential predicates and intrinsic properties first and of themselves belong; but all of these things are not constructed by the understanding, nor do they consist in some extrinsic denomination arising from an act of the intellect; therefore, the nature in things themselves has some universality which is the reason and basis of all these things. And this is confirmed, since we could otherwise scarcely avoid our falling into the opinion of the nominalists who deny that there are universal natures in reality, but say there are merely singular things, since, if the nature in reality has no universality, and if it is not distinguished 'ex natura rei' from the individuals, as was shown above, it is not clear what could immediately correspond in the real things to the common terms or their concepts besides the singulars themselves, as the nominalists teach, and consequently there could be no science of common things, but only of terms, as they also maintain.

7. The second opinion is that the nature existing in individuals is not actually universal, but nevertheless by no means derives its being universal from the intellect alone but rather is actually universal of itself and prior to any operation of the intellect and prior to any contradiction to individuals, and moreover, prior to any existence whether in the intellect or in fact itself. Fonseca treats and defends the opinion extensively in Book 5, *Metaphysics,* Ch. 28, throughout the first five questions. We shall examine the basis of this opinion afterward when we are supporting the true opinion; for this view is the middle ground between the two others and it takes arguments from each, partly to refute them and partly to urge and support itself.

8. The third opinion is that natures become actually universal only through the operation of the intellect, although there is some antecedent basis on the part of the things themselves on account of which the things may be said on their own part to be universal in potency. This is the common opinion of the ancient and modern philosophers; with Aristotle it is given very often in his books on *Metaphysics,* especially in Book 7; and the commentator in I *de Anima Com.* 8, says: "it

[43]

is the intellect which makes the universals in things"; and Avicenna, who spoke in this manner at the beginning of Book 5 of his *Metaphysics* "Horseness of itself is merely horseness, not one or many"; and St. Thomas speaks in the same way in *De Ente et Essentia,* Ch. 4, where he says, "the nature of itself is neither universal nor singular"; and in other places he speaks in the same way: "the intention of universality is derived from the intellect," as in *Ia,* q. 95, a.1; and *Ia, II ae,* q. 29, a.6; and 7 *Metaphysics,* Lec. 13; and all his disciples agree on that view: Cajetan, *loc. cit. Commentary on Being and Essence;* Soncinas and Javellus, cited in the previous section; Soto in his *Logic* q.2 *De Universalibus,* and others.

Resolution of the Question

9. Without doubt this last opinion is true. In order for us to explain and support it, the two things which we proposed in the title of the question must be made clear; first, in what way the unity which is necessary to the universality of a nature differs from formal unity; secondly, how the disposition to being in many things accrues to a nature which is thus one. From these there is established a third, specifically, the manner in which the universality of the nature can not be found in the things themselves. However, I assume something Aristotle often taught, that the nature of universality as such consists in two things, namely, in unity and in communicability. These two are included in that definition according to which the universal is called "one in many and of many" or "beyond many," which is taken from various places of Aristotle, I *Perihermenias,* Ch. 5; 1 *Post,* Chapter 18; 7 *Metaphysics,* Ch. 13. For, if the nature were not in some way one, then it would not be universal at all, but would be a multitude or aggregate of things; if, however, it were not disposed to be in many, it would not be universal, but singular; and it is indeed necessary that it be in many things in a manner opposed to singularity or individuality, that is, that it be in many inferiors which can be multiplied and ennumerated under this common notion. Therefore, these two, unity and community, are to be explained in such a way that it will be clear that the aspect peculilarly constitutive of the universal is not to be found in things apart from the intellect.

10. I say first: that formal unity of itself alone is not enough for the unity which the universal nature, insofar as it is universal requires and is accorded, but that another and greater unity is required. This is proved first, since the unity of a universal thing, inasmuch as it is universal, ought to be such as to be peculiar to it, and such as could not belong to a singular thing insofar as it is singular; but formal unity is not of this kind; therefore it, as such, is not enough for the unity of the universal nature as such. The major premise stands from the com-

mon agreement of everyone and from the opposition which there is between the singular and the universal as such; for when they are opposed as communicable and incommunicable, that unity which is indifferent to both of them cannot be enough for the nature of the universal, as will be further established from the following reasoning. The minor premise stands upon what has already been said about formal unity; for it was shown that it[10] was of itself indifferent to the nature either universally conceived or contracted into individuals. It is proved secondly since formal unity is multiplied in the individuals with the nature itself; but the unity which is peculiar to the universal nature, as universal, cannot be multiplied in inferiors; rather, they are one under this aspect, as Porphyry said: "By participation in the species, several men are one man"; therefore, the universal nature as such has another kind of unity besides formal unity. The major premise is proved above.[11] For we have shown that any individual nature is in itself formally one by a proper and intrinsic formal unity distinct from that which is in another similar nature, because each is in itself formally undivided through that which is in itself. And from here the minor proposition is easily proved, since if the unity of the universal nature insofar as it is universal were multiplied in inferiors, then the specific unity would be multiplied in individuals or the generic unity in the species, which is impossible; otherwise several men would be several species and each of them would have the unity of universality in itself, and consequently each would be universally one, just as it is formally one— something which is obviously false. So I argue thirdly, that since formal unity bespeaks only the formal or essential undividedness of that thing which is thus said[12] to be one, it is thus irrelevant to that unity whether the thing be singular or common; but universal unity indeed, intrinsically, bespeaks undividedness of several things in that thing or aspect which is denominated universally one, so that none of those inferiors which are contained under such a notion, taken by itself has that whole universal unity, but all the things are one under that notion. In this manner all species of animals are one in the notion of animal; no species, however, taken by itself has in itself the *universal* unity of "animal" which is quasi-potential, although it does have of itself its *formal* unity. Although formal unity is prerequisite for universal unity and is its basis, it is not by itself enough, but universal unity adds something beyond this.

11. You may say: Then, what or of what kind can this unity of the universal nature, as such, be? For every unity, as was implied above,

---

10 The "it" refers to "formal unity."
11 This Disputation, section I, number 11, "tot multiplicari unitates formales, quot sunt individua."
12 Literally: "denominated one."

[45]

must be either formal or numerical, since every division is either formal or material; but a universal unity cannot be numerical unity because this is proper to singular things; if, therefore, it is not formal, what can it be? The reply is that there is a unity distinct from these, having its own name and its own notion. This unity is called universal unity, and its notion consists in the undividedness of a certain nature into several natures alike in the same name and notion, and in its having a disposition to be divided into them. So unity of this kind includes both, namely, undividedness and the disposition to be divided into several things having the same name and notion, or which are such that it contains and includes in itself each one of them totally divided as to its actuality. Whence this undividedness closely approaches proper privation, since it bespeaks the negation of division in a nature disposed to such division. In this respect this unity differs from individual unity which not only bespeaks undividedness but also an inaptitude for division into many things which are the same kind as is that which is itself divided. It differs from formal unity because that unity, although not incompatible with that disposition or communicability to many things, does not require it. Whence, in God formal unity along with incommunicability to several natures is intelligible. Therefore, when it is said that every unity is either formal or numerical, it is true of the unities which belong in things themselves in their own regard or in reality itself. Besides these, there can be another unity which is produced through the understanding; and universal unity is of this kind, as we shall show.

12. Whence it is further added that this unity can be reduced to a numerical unity, which nevertheless is not simply real, but is of-reason or objective.[13] This is clarified; for the human species, in its notion of species is so one, that with others it composes the third or fourth, etc., of the species contained under "animal";[14] however, every unity which can complete a number can be spoken under the same numerical notion. Because of this, although "man" and "horse" absolutely differ essentially and in species, nevertheless they differ in number under the aspect of universals or species. Again, the formal concept of "man" as such, is one in number; whence its object, under the aspect of object, can also be said to be one in number, and thus a man in as much as he is considered as an example of that concept, is said to have objective numerical unity, either under the aspect of object (which is also a

13 The "objective concept" is the *thing-as-conceived;* hence, all properties or attributes or essences, as conceived by the mind are said to be "objective."

14 This is to remind the reader that the terms "man," "animal," and "horse" occur in this section in *simple supposition.* These uses become more frequent as the disputation progresses.

unity of reason), or through extrinsic denomination[15] based upon the concept of the mind; this unity is therefore necessary to the notion of the universal and under this aspect universal unity can be reduced to numerical unity. This can be explained in the following way also: for if we imagine that universals are things separate from individual things, according to the opinion of Plato as it was explained by Aristotle, then "man" as such would necessarily be understood, subsisting in itself, to be something itself transcendentally numerable with the others, and thus one in number although simultaneously it is imagined as existing in many things distinct in number (that this otherwise involves an absurdity, as has been said, is not pertinent to the present consideration for here we only intend to clarify the claim that the universal, in the way in which it exists or is apprehended, must be understood as undivided in itself and numerical either after the manner of a thing, if it is imagined as separate in reality, or after the manner of a notion or concept, if it is only mentally abstracted).

13. THERE IS NO UNIVERSAL UNITY PRIOR TO THE OPERATION OF THE MIND

On the basis of the preceding, I say secondly that the unity of the universal nature, as universal, is not real, nor is it in things in so far as they exist in reality itself and precede every operation of the understanding. This conclusion clearly follows from what has preceded, since no unity can be understood to be in real things besides formal and material unity; neither of these is sufficient for the notion of the universal as such. Perhaps it may be said that not only the formal unity by which each human nature, for instance, is said to be formally one, is found in things, but that there is also found a unity by which all human natures are said to have the same formal notion and consequently the formal unity by reason of which they share the same definition and by reason of which all men (from the point of view of the thing)[16] are said to be of the same nature. But on the contrary, this is not really unity, but merely similarity; for nothing is truly one and undivided in reality (from the point of view of the thing) in this and is that human nature, but there is merely something in this one to which something is similar in the other nature; however, this is not real unity but similarity. Whence, several things can be called, on the part of the thing, "of the same nature," that is, alike; for when this identity is said to obtain between distinct things, it cannot in fact be anything beyond a similarity, by reason of which they are also said to share or to have

---

[15] This term is explained in the introduction, pages 8-10.

[16] The Latin is: "*a parte rei.*" The expression, connoting "in reality independently of the operations of the mind" is idiomatic and receives various translations herein, as they best seem to fit the context.

[47]

the same definition, *fundamentally* indeed by reason of the mentioned similarities, *formally*, however, through reason, for definition is the work of reason.

14. THE REAL RELATION OF SIMILARITY IS NEITHER SUFFICIENT NOR NECESSARY TO THE NOTION OF THE UNIVERSAL

However, this similarity is simply neither necessary nor sufficient to the notion of the universal. I understand that it is not necessary with regard to the actual existence and relation [of things] because it is not part of the notion of the universal that it *actually* be in many things; for if the ideas of Plato were true, universals would exist of themselves, although no other individual actually existed, and as a matter of fact the natures of heaven and of Gabriel are universals, whether several of those individuals exist in reality having the aforementioned similarity among themselves or not. If, however, one speaks of that similarity as being *in potency,* then it *is* necessary to the nature of universality, because the nature could not otherwise be understood as common, as we shall explain more fully in a moment. However, that that similarity is not *sufficient* to the notion of the universal is proved because by force of that similarity taken all alone, whether in act or in potency, nothing is conceived as one thing common to many, but many things are conceived as alike among themselves; however, the universal as such must be conceived as one. Again, the universal, as universal, is conceived as actually undivided, insofar as it is such, and as dispositionally divisible and communicable; however, things insofar as they are really *similar* in nature, are actually divided and dispositionally or fundamentally "unifiable" (as I say) in one nature universally conceived.

15. And here the conclusion proposed is more extensively confirmed. For universality as such implies some undividedness, otherwise it would not be universality but merely multitude; but that cannot be the undividedness which belongs to things as they are in themselves, but only as they undergo conception by the mind; therefore the unity, which arises thence, is not real but of-reason. The minor is clarified, for as Aristotle rightly says in 7 *Metaphysics,* Ch. 14, and often in other places, to be in reality undivided and simultaneously to be actually divided into several things of the same name and notion, involves absurdity, for if a thing is really undivided[17] then it is really singular and one in number—which cannot happen. And this absurdity follows from the position of Plato, but disappears if the universal is understood to have undividedness only with regard to reason; since to be undivided with respect to reason and divided with respect to the thing, are not mutually opposed. And in this way all men are called on ac-

---

[17] In this case the expression "*a parte rei*" has been translated as "really."

[48]

count of the species, one man, since they are not divided in the concept of "man" as such, and thus the unity of "man," in so far as it is universal, is formed through reason, since "man," as such, has undividedness only insofar as it is the subject of the conception of the mind. This undividedness consists in the fact that "man," for instance, abstractly conceived, is not communicable to many men or to many objective concepts thus abstracted, although it is communicable through contraction to many individuals.

Section III

Whether the Common Nature of Itself Has Any Unity of Precision Outside of Individuals and Prior to the Operations of the Mind

1. Before we reply to the arguments for the opposite opinion, an objection which occurs here must be treated, and a certain opinion which seemed to me almost new and singular. And so it can be objected against the preceding resolution [of the question] that some common nature, for instance, human nature, not only insofar as it has been abstracted through the intellect but also insofar as it prescinds in itself from individual differences, and is by order of nature prior to those individual differences, has a certain unity; for, as such, it is not many, but only one; however, that unity, when it belongs of itself to the nature, will be real; therefore, that unity suffices for the notion of the universal. On this matter, Fonseca thinks (book 5, *Metaphysics*, Ch. 28, q. 3, sects. 2, 3, and 4) a certain unity belongs to the universal nature so taken, which it does not communicate to its inferiors, but which belongs to it alone and in isolation, prior to its existing either in the nature of things or in the understanding; he says this unity is distinct from formal unity because the latter is multiplied in individuals and the former is not. He calls that unity "unity of precision" or "numerical unity," not simply and absolutely, but "of the common nature," which is a diminishing condition, whence he also calls it a mixture somehow of formal and numerical unity. And as being of this opinion, he cites St. Thomas, Opusc. 42 *De Natura Generis*, Chapters 7 and 8, where he indicates that there are universal natures having some unity belonging to the nature taken absolutely, which is not communicated to the individuals of such a nature and which does not accrue to the nature through the understanding. He also cites Soncinas, 7 *Metaphysics* q.40, where he says that the nature considered in itself, that is, neither as it is in individuals nor as it is in the understanding, has some unity (and he does not seem to be speaking of formal unity because he

[49]

adds that the nature does not communicate this unity to its inferiors); and Capreolus thinks the same thing (in 3, d.5, q.5 art. 3, in his continuation of the argument of Scotus' first conclusion), where he affirms this, not of all universals but of some (from St. Thomas, *loc. cit.*), namely, of those which have not only logical but also physical unity and agreement. This limitation makes the matter more difficult and obscure, since it is impossible to find a universal unity not based on formal unity, as is established enough by what has been said and will more amply be clarified in what is coming. If one supposes formal unity, however, there remains the same argument with regard to every other unity in any universal nature whatever, since every such nature can be considered by itself and absolutely, and as such the same non-repugnance, indifference, or undividedness is found in whatever one you choose; and, hence Fonseca does not admit that limitation, but ascribes this unity of precision generally to all universal natures.

2. If you should ask where or when this unity accrues to such a nature, he will reply that an existing nature never has unity of this kind, since when it is contracted to individuals it does not have it; yet a nature has existence only in individuals; nor [he would say] does it even accrue to it as it is in the understanding, since it belongs to it by itself, before it is understood to have anything by the intellect; nor does it accrue to it only by extrinsic denomination, but it accrues through a true negation or undividedness belonging to the nature by itself. And Soncinas, above, thinks this too and consequently says this unity is not actual but potential. And both explain this through this conditional: if the nature were to exist without contraction to individuals, it would have this unity. You might again object that if this unity belongs *per se* to the nature taken absolutely, it will be inseparable from it, for what belongs *per se* to something always belongs to it and it is not possible that its opposite should belong to it; but the nature as found in individuals does not have that unity, but rather has the opposed multitude; therefore it is not possible that that unity belong *per se* to such a nature. They would reply that *"per se"* or *"secundum se"* can be understood in two ways: first, as it connotes the necessary connection of a predicate with the subject, as "being of the essence of its existent," or as "of something remaining intrinsically by it"; Aristotle takes it in this way when he enumerates the two senses of *"per se"* in I *Post*, Ch. 4; and in this sense the argument correctly proves that the mentioned unity does not belong *per se* to the nature of the universal. *"Per se"* is employed in another way for that which exists "absolutely" or "singly,"[18] and in this sense this unity is said to belong

---

[18] Literally: "in solitude" from the Latin: *"solitarie."*

to the nature through itself or taken by itself;[19] since, when that nature is considered absolutely or singly, that is, insofar as it does not have adjunct differences contracting it or individuating it, it will immediately have that unity. For it is not necessary that for something to belong to a nature in the latter sense of "taken by itself," that it also belong to it *"per se"* in the former sense, that is, intrinsically and necessarily; for many predicates, especially negative ones, can belong to a nature contingently when it is thus taken, such as "not to exist," "not to be generated," "not to be destroyed," "not to be white," "black," or all like predicates which do not belong to a common nature except on account of the individuals. Therefore, this unity of precision which consists in negation or privation belongs to the nature by itself and considered absolutely because, as such, the differences by which it is contracted and divided do not belong to it; nevertheless, it does not belong to the nature *per se* and necessarily, since the opposite can accrue to it through the mediation of its inferiors.

3. The Refutation of the Preceding Opinion

Nonetheless this opinion cannot be proved to me, for (as I omit its being clearly contrary to the opinions of St. Thomas in *De Ente et Essentia*, Ch. 4, and to that of Cajetan in the same place and to the opinions of the other authors cited already and to be referred to below in conclusion 4),[20] I do not sufficiently understand what kind of unity would belong to a nature prior to the understanding and nevertheless could never belong to it as found in its inferiors, or in it when it is existing in singulars; for, if that unity belongs to the nature prior to its understanding, then it is real unity; therefore it can sometimes really belong to that nature; it follows that it must be possible for it to belong to that nature in individuals or in some individual; for nothing really belongs to any nature unless it can belong to it as existing in some individual. For, it does not seem possible to understand what they say: that this unity belongs to the nature really with regard to the being of the essence but not with regard to the being of existence; because, as I have said above in treating of the concept of being and will say again below when treating of the essence and existence of creatures, the being of the essence cannot be conceived as real, unless it includes at least by disposition an order to existence; therefore, if this unity cannot belong to the essence as of an existent, neither will it belong to it as disposed toward existing; just as it would not exist except as an individual, so also it is not disposed toward existing except

---

[19] Literally: "taken through itself" from the Latin: *"per se."*

[20] It is difficult to decide exactly what passage Suarez is referring to here since no section is called "Conclusion 4"; there is some probability that the authors he has in mind are those cited in Section V, Number 1.

as an individual; therefore, the unity in no way really belongs to it. And this is confirmed, because no predicate, whether positive or negative, belongs to a nature taken by itself and alone, unless it either belongs to it by itself secondarily, or can belong to individuals; but this unity does not belong to the nature by itself in the manner mentioned, as they themselves admit; nor can it even accrue to the nature by reason of the individuals, since as such it is even more incompatible with it; rather, by the very fact that it is considered as it is found in individuals, it is already not being considered by itself and alone; therefore, in no way does it belong *"per se primo."* The major is supported by Porphyry, chap. *De Commun.*, St. Thomas, Cajetan, and others in the places mentioned. And it is obvious by induction with regard to negative predicates also (for there is no reason for doubting it about positive predicates), since *"not to be white, or black,"* etc. insofar as they belong to man as such, can belong to any individual of "man"; and more, that he should not exist, although it cannot belong to "man" by reason of any existing individual, belongs to "man" nevertheless insofar as some or all individuals of human nature do not exist. The reason is that these predicates are contingent and do not belong to the species except by reason of the individuals.

4. *An objection is answered.* If someone should object that there are certain negative predicates which belong to the common nature of itself, and which nevertheless do not belong to the individuals, as these seem to be: "not to be generated," "not to be destroyed," (for it is incompatible with the universal nature, taken alone, to be generated or to be created or even to exist), it must be answered that this is a sophistical equivocation; for the meaning of those negations can be multiple. The first is that the abstracted nature is neither generated nor corrupted nor can be, and in this sense those negations are true; nevertheless, if they are properly understood, they are not to be attributed to the nature taken by itself and absolutely but to the nature as having a certain status which it can have only through the understanding; for there is really no nature thus abstracted and alone, but it is considered by the intellect and to it, thus considered, such a negation is attributed. For this reason it is no wonder that it does not belong to the nature in individuals, since that status by reason of which such a negation belongs to the nature is destroyed through existence in individuals. Whence, if this unity of precision is to be compared with the negations, it will rather be precluded thereby from belonging to the nature except insofar as it undergoes the operation of the understanding abstracting and separating it. The other sense of those negations is that the common nature absolutely is neither generated nor corrupted and this can be understood to mean *either:* that it is not

generated in any way; and this is false, for it is at least secondarily generated and exists in individuals. *Or:* that it is not generated of itself primarily but by reason of the individuals; and this is true; nevertheless, this can also be said of the nature as it exists in individuals, as Aristotle says secondary substances exist in primary substances and by reason of them, and consequently not of themselves primarily. Whence, this negation taken in this sense does not belong to the nature contingently but of itself and necessarily; just as, on the other hand, "to be" and "to become" belong of themselves primarily to individuals if they must belong to anything. Therefore no contingent predicate, even a negative one, belongs to common natures unless either by reason of individuals (or in the individuals themselves), or by reason of the status which the common natures have in the intellect.

5. Finally I argue in this way against the opinion mentioned: the common nature is not *ex natura rei* distinguished from the individuals but is distinguished only through the intellect; therefore, it cannot have any unity by itself which it does not have in individuals, unless it be through the understanding. The antecedent has been proved frequently; the inference is proved first because the real "one" follows being; therefore, if the nature of itself does not have entity distinct from the entity of the individuals, neither can it have real unity distinct from the unity of the individuals; therefore it can have no unity of itself which it does not have in individuals; but every other unity is through the understanding. The same inference is proved, secondly, from the very terms which are employed in the other opinion; for it calls this unity, unity of "precision"; if, therefore, the precision is not in reality, neither does it accrue to the nature by itself, but only through the understanding; and neither can the unity accrue to the nature by itself also, if one excludes the understanding. Rather, if one rightly considers the matter, the very thing which is called "secundum se" in the sense explained above, involves the operation of the intellect because the nature is not *isolated* or separated from all individual differences except through the operation of the understanding. Whence, whatever accrues to the nature taken by itself, properly and peculiarly by reason of that condition or status which is explained by the particle "by itself"[21] in the sense given, accrues to it through the understanding; the aforementioned unity is of this kind, as has been shown.

6. *It is defended from a calumny.* Hence it is understood, by the way, that no equivocation is committed by St. Thomas, Cajetan, and the others (as Fonseca thinks) when they say that whatever belongs to a nature by itself or through itself belongs to it as it exists in individuals, since whatever belongs to a thing of itself, always belongs to

---

[21] Latin: *"secundum se."*

it; for in both places they use "per se" in the same sense, namely "secondarily," as indeed it must be taken. And similarly, [there is no equivocation] when these same writers distinguish three ways in which something belongs to a nature, namely, either as it exists in individuals, or as it is in the understanding, or *of itself*,[22] namely: for that which of itself and intrinsically belongs to a nature, and not by reason of any state of contraction or of isolation or abstraction. For, it supposes that nothing can belong to a nature proximately and immediately, insofar as it is such a nature, unless it belongs to it through itself (something we have shown to be true), and on the contrary that whatever belongs contingently to the common nature belongs to it by reason of the state of individuation which it has in reality or of separation which it has through the understanding. Whence, as the equivocation is clearly removed, every predicate which is said immediately (as I say) of the common nature, that is, not because of the individuals, can be said to belong to it through itself; yet this predicate can be of two kinds; one belonging to the nature precisely as having such a formal notion, as "to be a rational animal" and consequently, "to be risible," "to be admiring," etc.; and predicates of this kind are said to belong to the nature most properly by itself and of itself, that is, from the fact that it is precisely this kind of nature. And St. Thomas and the others are talking in this way of the nature by itself[23] when they distinguish two of its states, namely: in individuals and in the understanding; and they rightly conclude that whatever belongs to the nature by itself in this way, belongs to it whenever and however it exists. Other predicates can be said to belong to a nature of itself, that is, taken in common, yet not because of the nature itself, but because of this isolation and separation which that particle "of itself" [secundum se] indicates. And such consideration of a nature coincides with the state which the nature has through the understanding, and those predicates likewise coincide with the attributes which accrue to that nature because of this state; otherwise, it would be necessary to employ a fourth consideration of the nature besides the triple consideration recently explained—which is unheard of. When that unity is said, therefore, to belong to a nature of itself, yet not because it is *such* a nature, but precisely because it is taken or considered *by itself*, it obviously proves conclusively that that unity does not belong to the nature except with respect to the status which it has in the understanding.

7. Thirdly, the same main conclusion of the argument is further proved and emphasized, since an actually existing nature is not distinguished from the individual *ex natura rei*, and hence, as such, cannot have a real unity incompatible with individuation—of which

22 *Ibid.*   23 *Ibid.*

kind common unity is; but the common nature taken as possible or according to the being of its essence, is not distinguished *ex natura rei* from the individuals taken also as possible beings, or according to the being of the individual essence; therefore, for the same reason some unity incompatible with individual unity cannot belong to such a nature by itself and prior to understanding; the unity of isolation or common numerical unity would be of this kind. The major premise is established by what has been said and is not denied by the others. The minor is easily proved since the relation of possible things among themselves is the same as that of existents among themselves because other things than what are possible do not exist or come into being. Nor does possible humanity have an essence different from what it has when it exists; therefore if humanity as such, when it actually exists, is not distinguished *ex natura rei* from this or that humanity, neither is humanity as possible distinguished *ex natura rei* from this or that possible humanity. Moreover, if we speak correctly, humanity is not possible except insofar as this and other individual humanities are possible, just as there exists no humanity except insofar as individual humanity exists. The inference is indeed proved by the same reason and relation since there is no humanity possible in reality and apart from the understanding other than this or that humanity; therefore incompatible unities cannot belong to it. And this is confirmed; for if this unity belongs to the nature, prior to the understanding, to which nature, I ask, does it belong? To the singular? And this is not so, as is self-evident and as they admit. Does it belong to the common nature insofar as it is common? And this is not so, since there is no such nature, even possibly, if we take away the activity of the understanding. Or to the nature, as nature with nothing else being added even by the intellect? This also is not so, since as such the nature has only the formal unity which is communicated to individuals and multiplied in them; therefore, apart from the understanding there can be no adequate subject and basis for such a unity.

8. *The basis of the opposed opinion is overthrown.* The difficulty is answered, therefore, by our denying what is assumed in it, namely, that human nature, for instance, has some unity of itself which is distinct from formal unity. However, that objection starts from a false principle, namely, that the specific nature of itself prescinds from individuals by some real isolation[24] or an isolation which belongs to it by

[24] Literally: "precision." For purposes of linguistic felicity I have translated what is literally "unity of precision" into "unity of isolation" in various contexts that follow. The English word "isolation" is used in this text only in cases where it translates the Latin "precisio." In a few cases the verb "prescind" is used, since we have no intransitive form for "isolate."

nature; when in fact, it does not prescind except through the intellect abstracting and conceiving the common nature apart from individuals, the basis of which precision is indeed in the nature itself; but this is not other than the formal unity which is multiplied in individuals and is in them through identity. Also it appears that another falsehood is supposed in the objection, namely, that the specific nature for instance, is by order of nature prior to the individuals, and as such has that unity of isolation or common numerical unity; for if the discussion be concerned with real priority, that is, priority based upon some real causality or disposition or real order, it is not true since where there is no distinction *ex natura rei,* there cannot be a real order or causality. Then also, such a priority is intelligible neither in the notion of the thing existing nor in the being of its essence. It is obvious first that if there is any order, it is rather that the specific nature exists because some individual of it exists, as Aristotle said of primary and secondary substances. It is obvious secondly, since the being of the essence isolated from the existence is nothing other than the entity of the thing in possible being, as will be shown below; however, we have proved that even universals are possible in this way by reason of possible singulars. If "the being of the essence" is taken to refer to the quidditative predicates taken in isolation and abstracted from the individuating differences, then "the being of the essence" in this sense involves the operation of reason conceiving the common notion in which the individuals agree, abstracted from their peculiar differences. Indeed, if the common essence, taken in this sense, is called prior in nature, not with a proper and real priority, but with that priority which is said to be the result of underlying [the individuals], then that is rather a priority of reason; for it involves the concept of the mind which abstracts the common notion from the singulars; whence being prior in this manner is nothing other than being more universal. However, from this priority, it is not possible that some numerical unity which belongs to the nature of itself prior to the individual and every intellect, be collected; therefore there is no such unity unless through reason and the concept of the mind, as we have said in the Conclusion [No. 5, above].

9. But it can be objected against what has been said that the universal nature as such cannot be said to be one in number, under the aspect of universal, through extrinsic denomination from the formal concept of the mind, namely: because it is represented through a concept one in number; therefore it must be called one in number under the aspect of universal by some other unity which precedes in the nature itself and is represented through that concept; therefore such a unity accrues to the nature of itself and not through the understanding. The first antecedent is clear first because it is rather the case that a con-

cept has unity from the object, than the converse; therefore it is not the case that the object is one because the concept is one, but the converse. Secondly, because otherwise the same nature represented by different men in distinct concepts would be many universals in number, for if the forms giving the unity are multiplied, the unity will be multiplied. The consequent is, however, plainly false; for we would not say that human species are several in number because human nature is represented in several concepts; just as there are not several faces of Christ the Lord because it is represented in several images; therefore just as several concepts do not bestow plurality upon a universal nature, so neither does one concept bestow unity, but rather supposes it; therefore this unity we are talking about is not produced by reason but belongs to the nature of itself, seeing that it is objectionable in the case of several similar concepts.

10. It can be replied, only to be proved, that formal unity belongs to the nature of itself, and that it is supposed to the concept of the mind, and by reason of that, human nature, for instance, can have the status of one object with respect to the concept of the one abstracting and isolating it, and because that status is not multiplied, even if formal concepts of the same nature are multiplied, the universal of this kind is therefore simply not multiplied in number, insofar as it is universal. But on the other hand, formal unity alone is not enough to render this universal one in number unless something else be added, since such unity is common to individual things and is multiplied in them; therefore, besides formal unity, another unity is necessary by which the common nature as such is called one in number under the aspect of universal; for nothing can be designated one in number except from a unity which is numerical under that aspect, and this is what the argument is about. As human nature, for example, is called a species one in number; it cannot therefore have that unity from its formal unity as such, since Peter has a like formal unity and is not such a species; therefore there is another unity of human nature which is incommunicable to individuals, by which human nature is called one species. Either it has that unity from the concept of the mind, and thus this unity is multiplied when the concept is multiplied as the argument made above contends, or it is not produced through the concept, and thus belongs to the nature of itself, as the opposing opinion was claiming. It is answered, while further clarifying the response given, that it is indeed true that formal unity does not suffice for universal unity, or for the nature to be called one universal in number; but there is necessary the isolation by the mind, by reason of which the unity incommunicable to individuals accrues to the nature thus abstracted, which unity consists in: undividedness or incommunicability to several

natures thus abstracted and common, along with a disposition to be communicated to several contracted natures or individuals; this negation or incommunicability is not multiplied in the nature even if the formal concepts are numerically multiplied, and on that account it is not necessary that, because of several formal concepts distinct in number, the nature conceived should be said to be several numerically distinct universals.

11. Therefore, the reply to the objection is put in proper form by denying the first antecedent in the sense already explained. It is replied to the first proof that for the unity of the formal concept it is enough that the fundamental unity of the objective concept be supposed on the part of the object, which unity consists in the similarity or agreement of several singulars in formal unity; for this is enough for the intellect by its own power and efficacy of understanding to be able to abstract the common objective concept; whence, with regard to this isolation of such a common and universal object, the intellect does not suppose the object itself but makes or rather confers on it that state of isolation through extrinsic denomination. To the second proof it is answered that the form by which the nature is thus properly denominated one, is not the very concept of the mind but is the negation of incommunicability to several natures thus common, which negation is founded in the abstraction of the mind; this negation is the same, however, whether this abstraction is made through one or through various formal concepts distinct in number.

12. For otherwise it could be said that, although in the abstract the intentions of universality are multiplied through the multiplication of formal concepts concerning the same nature (in this manner the dialecticians are accustomed to say that a numerically distinct "relation of reason" to the nature of the species arises in human nature through the distinct comparison of it to individuals, made by Peter and Paul or by the same person at different times), nevertheless, the universal is simply not multiplied in the concrete, since that which underlies such a notion of universality is formally not multiplied but is taken up as having exactly the same formal unity with the same isolation. Just as, although several whitenesses, distinct in number, can inhere in the same man, he is not said to be several white things but one; and likewise, although what is in the eye is constituted by the notion of what is seen or named from vision, it is not called several things seen, but one even though it appears at once to several visions; for in concrete things of this kind, the unity is taken from what is supposed, either from the subject or from what serves as subject. In the present case, however, the nature which is denominated universal, serves as subject with regard to the intention of universality, and on

that account, even though the forms or denominating concepts are multiplied, the universal is not multiplied, since all these things [denominating concepts] turn on the same nature, and they isolate it with respect to the same formal unity.

SECTION IV

What the Disposition In the Universal Nature for Being In Many Things Might Be

1. A reason for doubting is found sufficiently in what was said in the two preceding sections and especially in the arguments proposed in section 2; this doubt has been put forward to dismiss that argument more clearly.

2. *The disposition to being in many is nothing in the nature, insofar as it exists on the part of the thing.* Therefore I say first: the disposition of the common nature to have being in many things is not something belonging to the nature itself insofar as it exists on the part of the thing. This is the most "received" of conclusions, as seems obvious, especially if we suppose what has often been said, that the universal is not distinguished *ex natura rei* from the singulars or inferiors. It is proved because on the part of the thing there is nothing except what is singular and individual, and in the singulars themselves, nothing is distinct from them *ex natura rei*. In the nature, therefore, insofar as it exists on the part of the thing, there can be no disposition for being in many things. The consequence is obvious, since there is no such disposition or compatibility in an individual thing as such but rather there is the opposite incompatibility; the nature insofar as it exists in reality is individual and is in fact entirely indistinct from the individual. Some say that although there is no proximate potentiality for being in many things found in an existing nature, since as such the nature is contracted and determined to one thing, nevertheless there is a remote disposition since, with respect to itself if the contraction were removed, it could be communicated to many, just as prime matter, when existing under one form and under the dispositions appropriate to it, is not proximately disposed to other forms, and yet nevertheless retains its remote disposition toward them. But the example is not relevant since matter and its substantial disposition toward form is one in number and is a singular entity really distinct from form and from the disposition which it now has, which dispositions can lose this form and gain another; and as a result, it is no wonder that matter existing under one form should retain a radical disposition for receiving others. But the

[59]

common nature as contracted to this particular individual is not something distinct *ex natura rei* from the individual or from the contracting difference; nor can it happen that the same human nature (from the point of view of the thing), for instance, existing in Peter should lose the individuation which it has in Peter and gain another, and hence as it exists in reality the nature has neither a proximate nor a remote disposition for existing in many things, either simultaneously or successively.

3. Whence I argue secondly that every common nature as it exists in some individual in reality, is so determined to it [the individual] that the same nature (with regard to the thing) cannot be determined to another; therefore in no individual is it undetermined toward several individuals; "To be determined to this individual" and "to be undetermined toward several" are opposed contradictorily or privatively; therefore, in no individual does the nature have a real disposition for being in many things since this disposition cannot obtain without indifference; therefore, insofar as it exists in reality it absolutely does not have this aptitude since it does not exist except in the aforesaid manner, determined in individuals. You may say that it is not incompatible to be indifferent of itself, and yet determined through an individual difference; therefore the nature existing in individuals can have both. It is replied that whatever may be the case concerning the true meaning of that proposition, which was assumed: "the nature is of itself indifferent," and about which I shall speak in a moment, nevertheless it can only be construed to mean that the nature does not have a determination without an individual difference, and granted that this be so, nonetheless, after such an individual difference is bound to the nature, the nature thus contracted cannot actually remain indifferent. It can be said in sum that if it did not have that contraction it would be indifferent; yet since as a matter of fact it never exists without such contraction, then as a matter of fact it never exists indifferently or with a disposition to be indifferent.

4. It is thirdly maintained that the universal nature exists in many things only by identity with them singly; but such a nature identified with one individual cannot, while remaining the same both in essence and real existence, be identified with others; therefore such a nature, as it is communicated to individuals in reality, and as it exists in them cannot have a real disposition for being in many things. The major is certain, from what was said above, in which we showed that the universal is not distinguished from the singulars *ex natura rei*. Indeed, real identity is enough for the efficacy of the aforesaid reason; for by reason of that very identity, the genus already contracted to one species cannot, as the same genus in essence and real existence, be con-

tracted to another species. Therefore, with respect to genus, species and essential difference, the assumed major proposition is obvious since, because these are essential to their inferiors and are predicated essentially of them not in the manner of a part but in the manner of the whole (since a part is not predicated of the whole), it is necessary that they be in them by identity insofar as they are predicated of them (because nothing is more closely identified with a thing than its essence). One can hesitate over 'property' and "accident," since these do not seem to be in their inferiors through identity but through *information*.[25] But we are chiefly discussing the former universals; for the most proper unity of the universal nature is with respect to the inferiors which are contained essentially under it. Yet even in the case of property and accident, insofar as they are universal, the assumed proposition holds true. For a property and an accident do not have the status of a universal insofar as they are certain forms physically informing their subjects, both since they are considered under this aspect [i.e., as universal] only in the abstract, in a manner in which they are not predicated of their subjects; and also, since no property or accident is given in reality in this manner, which of itself might be universal with regard to informing several subjects. And, although with respect to the common notion of some property or accident, for example, "whiteness" or "risibility," the form can be called universal in some way with respect to such subjects, nevertheless this does not belong to this form, except insofar as its common aspect exists through identity in the singular forms informing such subjects. And in this way such a disposition for having being in many things is reduced to the mode of being in inferiors through identity. These things are properly called universal, insofar that, taken in the concrete, they are disposed to be predicated of their subjects and thus also are in them by identity not because of an accidental form, but because of the supposit. For one thing is truly predicated of many things and of single things only insofar as it is the same as they; for the proposition affirming "this" to be "that" requires for its truth some identity between predicate and subject since it is necessary that they stand for the same thing and that they either explicitly or implicitly signify the same thing. It is therefore true that every universal is in its inferiors through identity—which was the major proposition assumed. The minor was sufficiently proved in the preceding reasoning and is almost obvious from its terms since the specific nature, for example as it exists in reality, is so identified with each individual in which it exists that, insofar as it is in that individual, it cannot lose the identity with it and consequently cannot, as such,

[25] "Information" occurs here in its technical sense as the noun correlated with the function of a form to *inform* the things having that form.

have a real identity with others; therefore it is incompatible with such a nature that it have a disposition for being in many things through identity; so, because the act of being in many things through identity is of the nature of the universal, a real disposition to such an act is not compatibly found in the nature existing on the part of the thing.

5. A third reason can be added: that if this disposition is in the existing nature, then that same disposition also exists in reality; so, that disposition is also singular and individual; for whatever exists in reality is singular and individual; hence such a disposition will be in some individual nature; for it cannot exist separated through itself, but only in the nature, since it is its property and disposition. Because it is really existing and individual, it is necessary that it be in a really existing and individual nature, and consequently because there is no better reason why this should apply to one individual nature rather than the others, there will be such a disposition in all and each individual nature. From this many absurdities follow. The first is that there are as many universal human natures as there are natures contracted in the individuals, since each of these is in itself one, having its own and real disposition for being in many things, distinct from the disposition of another. For it cannot be imagined that the disposition for being in many things should be one in number in all the individual natures. Otherwise, it would also have to be said that the numerically same nature is contracted to the singular individual: than which nothing could be more absurd. The rest is obvious since a disposition is only in the nature; indeed it cannot be imagined as a thing distinct from the nature; therefore, if the disposition is numerically one in all, the nature will also be numerically one in all. Again, either [a] that disposition is called one in number as it were "collectively," so that it is not whole in the simple natures but in each one there is something of that disposition and from all of them there results one disposition to many things—and this is outside what has been put forward. For according to that explanation there is in each individual nature a disposition for being in itself, and no nature has an aptitude for being in many things. But if there be talk of "collection," as the whole collection of dispositions is considered as one, so also the whole collection of natures can be considered as one; indeed that nature as such, that is, as collectively one, is not in many things since the whole collection is not in the single individual natures, but is the aggregate of all; therefore this unity of the collection is irrelevant to the analysis of the universal, for it [the universal] ought to so exist in the many that it is entirely in each if them. Or [b] that disposition is simply one in itself and is whole in the singulars and in all the individuals and thus the same will have to be said of the nature itself for the same reason; and

[62]

it is not more inconvenient to admit this with regard to the nature itself than with regard to that disposition. It is obvious that both are completely foolish; this is much more so than to postulate numerically one accident simultaneously in different subjects; again absurdity is involved even in the terms when it is said that numerically the same nature is contracted to several individuals; since, if it is the same in number, then it is one in number and is individual, and is therefore incommunicable to many individuals. On the other hand, it follows that in each individual there is some real intrinsic disposition toward the individual difference of another individual; however, this is impossible because there cannot be a real disposition to that which is completely repugnant: but it is completely repugnant that something which is in me really and essentially, be contracted and individuated through the individual differences of another man; therefore there cannot be in me a real disposition toward this.

6. *The disposition to have existence in many things does not belong to the common nature of itself prior to the understanding.* I say secondly: the disposition to exist in many things is not some real property belonging to the common nature by itself prior to the operation of the intellect. This assertion can be proved by almost the same reasons through which we showed a little earlier that a nature by itself does not have unity of isolation[26] except through the intellect; for these two follow one another. For if a nature, as actually existing, is not really disposed to be in many things, it is because it does not exist except as contracted and determined to this or that individual; therefore such a disposition for being in many things cannot belong to the nature unless it be isolated from every contraction. Therefore if the nature does not have this isolation of itself but has it only through the understanding then neither will it have this disposition prior to every intellect. Secondly, if this disposition belongs to a nature by itself prior to every intellect, it belongs to the nature either as existing or as not existing; it does not belong to the nature as existing, as has been shown, since it does not exist unless made individual through identity; nor can it belong to a nature not existing, since in order for a nature which does not exist to be conceived as having this disposition, it must be conceived as at least possible, because to be able to be in many things intrinsically includes and supposes being *able* to be; however, it has been shown that the nature as possible is as much individual as the nature as existing; therefore it can no more be in the nature as possible than in the nature as existing.

---

[26] See note 24, above. Literally: "precision."

7. Thirdly: for I ask what this disposition might be. They reply that it is a certain positive mode belonging to the nature of itself, on which is based the non-repugnance to the nature that it should be in many things. Yet, [they say] this mode is not actual, but potential, that is, is such that it cannot belong to a nature which is actually existing, but only to a nature in potency or to one existing objectively. By which it also happens that such a mode is not entirely inseparable from the nature, but rather separable, since the nature when actually existing does not have such a disposition or such a mode of being. Just as (they say) the mode of being which a thing has in its causes is a real mode belonging to the things as long as they do not exist, which ceases to belong to them as soon as they are produced, since they are now said to be not in their causes but beyond their causes. But these things are not proved to me; for I do not satisfactorily conceive of a mode both real and positive and conceive that it should be impossible for it to exist in reality. For in that way in which something positive is called real, it is enclosed within the ambit of real being; there is no real being except with relation to the act of being; that with which the act of being is entirely incompatible cannot be contained within the ambit of real being; therefore it can be neither a thing nor a positive real mode. But, if it is not a real mode, it will be a mode of reason, and consequently it will not belong to the nature prior to the understanding. Besides, this also enforces the argument put forth above: that contingent predicates do not belong to a nature of itself but because of something added, perhaps the status which it has in reality or in the understanding; if therefore this disposition belongs to it of itself and not by reason of any status, then it will also belong to it through itself and not contingently; therefore it will belong to it inseparably, something they themselves properly deny, because it does not belong to the nature in individuals.

8. Next I ask about that disposition which is said to be conceived as a certain potential real mode, whether it is to be conceived as one in number or as merely one in species and multipliable in number. This latter cannot be said since it would be necessary to conceive of it as multipliable in individuals, which is absurd. The first also can scarcely be conceived; for how can a real disposition, one in number, be conceived as related to several distinct individual differences, when indeed there is none which can, being the same in number, be contracted in them all whether simultaneously or successively? But if it is said that the disposition is not one in number *simply*, but only *as it were*, namely, by common numerical unity, then it has already been shown that no such unity can be accounted for except through *reason*. Finally, that disposition either intrinsically follows the formal unity of

[64]

the specific nature or accrues to it from without. If the first is claimed, it follows that it cannot any more be one in number, than is formal unity itself which we have shown not to be one in number since it is multipliable in number. It also follows that the disposition is to be found wherever formal unity is found—which is false; otherwise it would be found in individuals. If the second is claimed, then it will have to be determined whence or from what principle or cause this disposition accrues to a nature having such a formal notion; it will have to be made clear, furthermore, in what state or under what condition, which obtains on the part of this nature and not on the part of the intellect, this nature is to be imagined or conceived, which nature is, as it were, an adequate subject for that disposition; and it will be clearly understood that neither of these can be explained except in relation to the abstraction and separation which is produced by the mind, since ignoring this, there is no common nature distinct *ex natura rei* from the individuals, whether in a state of actual existence or in a state of potential existence, or in the being of the essence or possible being, as has often been declared.

9. WHETHER THE MODE OF BEING IN THE CAUSE IS ANYTHING REAL IN THE EFFECT

However, that example of a potential mode, which it is claimed that things have in their causes before they exist, in no way assists the aforesaid opinion. First, because that mode, insofar as it is called real or thought to be real, is sometimes in reality, namely, wherever the thing is said to be in its cause. Next, because it is also the case that that mode either does not cease to be when the thing is produced beyond its causes or, on that part on which it ceases to be, it is not a positive mode but rather a privative mode. When a thing is said to have being merely in its causes, before it exists, two things are asserted: the first is that there is in the cause the power to give being to such a thing, which power, as it were by extrinsic denomination, denominates the effect to have being, not simply, but in the cause; and in this regard, such being in the cause is not lost, even if the thing is produced in itself and beyond the cause, because the power of the cause remains undisturbed. Another thing which is implied when it is said that a thing has being in its cause, is that it does not yet exist in itself, and this is what is lost when it is produced in itself; however this is not positive but privative, as is obvious. You may say that beyond these things there is a certain potential mode by which it is called possible, which mode is lost, by the fact that it begins to exist. It is answered that this is not a positive mode distinct from the aforementioned on the part of the effect because, as will be said below when we are treating essence and existence, the objective disposition of possible things toward existing is not on their own part, unless a certain non-repugnance also on the part of the cause denotes a potency for producing them. However, (what is relevant to the present matter) supposing we granted that the disposition is a positive mode, it would have to be claimed that when the thing is produced it does not lose that disposition insofar as it is positive, but only with regard to the lack of its act; for the thing, when it exists, is not less disposed to existing than it was before; but it merely has the act of existing which it did not have before; nor is it likely that it would lose a positive real mode precisely through the fact that it actually begins to exist.

10. I say thirdly: the disposition of a common nature to be in many things is only a certain indifference or non-repugnance which has its basis in the nature of itself; but it does not actually belong to it except insofar as it undergoes the abstraction of the intellect. This assertion is common; and on this the writers mentioned, especially Cajetan and the other Thomists, seem to agree. First, it must be clarified, next proved. That this indifference belongs to the nature of itself can be interpreted in two ways. First, that this non-repugnance belongs of itself to the nature by virtue of its formal unity. And in this sense, it is false; otherwise the non-repugnance or indifference (which is the same thing) would be inseparable from the nature, and consequently the nature as it exists in reality would have this non-repugnance, which is obviously false; for as it is in reality, it is intrinsically and through identity made individual so that it is incompatible with it that it should be in many things. In the other sense the assertion can be interpreted merely negatively, namely, that the nature by virtue of its formal unity, taken in isolation, does not have a repugnance to being in many things. And in this sense, it is true. From this the conclusion is easily clear with regard to both parts. For, in the first place, such non-repugnance, as it was explained, is based on the very formal unity which of itself is not individual, and in this way the nature can be said, even existing in things, to have this non-repugnance, for even in a thing itself it [the nature] is not incommunicable by force of its formal unity, but by force of its individual unity. Although the whole nature along with the formal unity which is in the individual is incommunicable, and although it is repugnant for it to be in many things, nonetheless it does not have the repugnance by virtue of the formal unity of the nature but by virtue of the individuation.

11. And hence the other part is confirmed, namely, that this disposition toward being in many things (even through the non-repugnance we have explained) does not belong to the common nature insofar as it exists on the part of the thing, insofar as it is necessary to the notion of the universal. For, in order for a nature to be universal, it is not

[66]

enough that by itself it should not have a determination to one thing, if otherwise, at least from the addition of an individual difference, it has it; but it is requisite that it be absolutely and simply indifferent. But as existing on the part of a thing it is not thus indifferent, rather, it is simply determined to one thing wherever it exists; therefore a nature, as it exists in reality, does not have indifference or non-repugnance. This is confirmed and illuminated: *repugnance* to being in many things belongs to an existing nature by reason of the individual difference; therefore for a nature to be *disposed* to being in many things through non-repugnance, is nothing else than to be disposed to existing in many things through abstraction or isolation from every individual difference; this isolation and abstraction does not belong to the nature as existing on the part of the thing, nor does it belong to it in any state which precedes any consideration of the understanding; because there is no state of this kind in which the nature of itself abstracts from individuals, either existing or possible, as was made clear above; therefore.

Finally, it is supported by an adequate enumeration of parts, that this disposition or non-repugnance does not belong to an existing nature of itself prior to any act of the understanding; so, it can only belong to it as undergoing the conception of the understanding. Especially since it has already been made clear that this non-repugnance or indifference consists in or arises from the separation of all differences of inferiors or individuals; however, this separation does not precede in any way in the nature itself, nor in the existing thing, nor in the nature taken in any state of possibility, but only insofar as it is objectively in the understanding; therefore. . . .

12. *Objection—Reply—Why several individuals can be under one species and not under another.* Someone will urge that the fact that several individuals can be multiplied under the same species does not result from the intellect but is based upon the very nature in the thing; therefore the disposition for having being in many things accrues to the nature of itself and not through the intellect. The inference is obvious since these two are either the same or follow one another in reality, namely, that individuals can be multiplied under the same species, and that the specific nature can be communicated to them. The antecedent, however, is clear, first from the fact that individuals are multipliable under the same species is not something fabricated through reason but is something grounded in the things themselves; secondly, from the fact, on the other hand, that if an angelic nature (as many wish) is not multipliable in number, this follows from some real and intrinsic property belonging to it (something which is most certainly the case in the divine nature). Therefore, conversely it is a real property belonging to it that human nature be multipliable in number

[67]

and it is not something excogitated by reason. It is answered that this argument leads to and strengthens the conclusion that the disposition to be in many things is fundamentally and remotely in things themselves (not, however, proximately), insofar as it expresses the indifference and indeterminacy of the common nature to one thing. However, "disposition," remote and proximate, is not employed by us in the sense in which some people (as I was saying above) assert that the disposition or potency is removed under an act in behalf of others and that the nature existing in the thing has this disposition; for we have sufficiently disproved this. But I call the remote basis of this disposition a natural condition or property of such a nature by reason of which multiplication of individuals within the same species is not incompatible with it; however, this property is not some disposition of the common nature as such, which is understood as a certain potency capable of actualization through several differences, but it is only a perfection and limitation of this kind of nature. Whence, this property, which underlies this indifference or non-repugnance, cannot be understood as isolated and in the common nature, but is also in the particulars themselves or individuals, as they are such. As, for example, in the human species, any individual is of such a condition that it is not incompatible to it to have another like it in species. And it is common to each and all individuals of that species that it is not incompatible that other things be alike only with respect to some genus and not in the species which accrues to them either from the fact that they are material or from the fact that they are finite substances (with which it is compatible that they should have among themselves some similarity or univocal agreement). Thus, it is rightly understood both that this disposition for being in many things has its basis in things themselves, and that such a basis is not some positive, common and indifferent disposition in reality itself, but is a limitation or a condition of things which are such that they include nothing in their own being by reason of which it is repugnant to them to have other things like them or equal to them in perfection. And finally, it is understood that this basis of indifference or non-repugnance is not to be imagined only in the common nature by itself, but in the individuals themselves and in singular things since, granted that the nature is determined in each individual to that individual alone, it is, nevertheless, in that thing in such a way that it is not by force of *that* repugnant that it be in another like thing or, rather, that a similar nature be in another individual; and this alone is a sufficient foundation for the indifference and disposition to have being in many things which belongs to the common nature as abstracted through the intellect; there is not some indetermination which the nature itself has by itself or in individuals.

[68]

13. *Reply.* Therefore, to the objection in form, I concede the antecedent, namely, that the fact that some individual things can be multiplied alike in species, is based on things themselves and not upon the operation of the intellect; however, I distinguish the consequent, namely, that the disposition toward being in many things belongs to the nature of itself. For it can be understood to be about a proximate disposition, that is, a disposition which is conceived by us in the manner of a certain capacity, isolated from all contracting differences and actualizable through them; and in this sense the inference is denied because such a capacity, preceding in nature in the thing itself, is not necessary in order for it to be possible that individuals be multiplied in the same species. But it is sufficient that there should be in individuals no property by reason of which it is incompatible with them that other things be like them. If, however, that consequent is understood to be about the remote basis in the aforementioned sense, the inference is thus conceded; yet it is not contrary to the things we have said, as is obvious. Whence, what is said in the proof of the inference, namely: "these two are the same: that individuals can be multiplied in the same species and that the specific nature can be communicated in them," is also equivocal. For in the multiplication of individuals of the same species there is not in reality any other communication of the nature than *assimilation* and a certain agreement among the individuals themselves; whence neither is there in the common nature by itself any other disposition to be communicated to many things than that there should be in the individuals a non-repugnance to having other things alike. If, therefore, by "communication of the specific nature" nothing else is meant, the whole argument is conceded and nothing is implied against what was said. Suppose however, (as the words more probably mean) "the nature can be multiplied in many things" is understood in terms of the above described disposition of a certain common nature which (although it be one) is conceived as spreading itself and communicating itself to many things—this is the work of reason and the manner of our understanding; for in reality there is nothing of this sort which precedes, nor is it necessary in order to account for the multiplication of things which resemble one another.

Section V

Whether the Unity of the Universal Arises from the Operation of the Intellect, and How It is Reconciled with the Difficulties Posed In Behalf of the Contrary View

1. Universality Is Through the Intellect with a Foundation in Reality.

From everything which has been said, a resolution of the problem of the unity of the universal and the answer to the arguments proposed in Section II, is easily put together. Thus, it must be claimed that the universal unity arises through the activity of the intellect, granting that the basis or occasion is taken from the singular things themselves. Also, it must be claimed that there is a certain unity of reason accruing to natures insofar as they are made objects of the mind and arising thence through denomination. I think this is the opinion of Aristotle in the places mentioned; and he says for this reason that: "the universal is either nothing or it is secondary," that is, contingent upon the operation of the intellect (I *De Anima*, text 8), just as St. Thomas, Albert the Great, and all the others understand him; and consequently the Commentator says here "the intellect makes the universality in things"; and in the *Commentary on the 12th Book of the Metaphysics*, number 4, he says: "according to Aristotle the universals are collected from particulars in the intellect which accepts the common similarity among them and makes from this, one notion"; and in Commentary 27 he says: "There is no demonstration made concerning the particular, although, in the truth of the matter, that alone is a real thing." This is also the opinion of St. Thomas in *Being and Essence*, Ch. 4, and the other places mentioned above; and St Thomas cites Avicenna, 5 *Metaphysics* Ch. 1. Also, all the Thomists agree on this: Capreolus, Cajetan, Soncinas, and the others cited above. Again, Durandus holds the same view in I *Sent.*, d.3, q.5; II *Sent.*, d.3, q.7; and Giles of Rome in I *Sent.*, q.2, Prolog, and d.19, q.1; and Scotus might possibly be construed into the same opinion, for his words are not incompatible when he says that in reality there is only the universal in potency, not in act; and thus, it seems, his disciples explain him, as Fonseca extensively refers to him and treats him (the work mentioned, cap. 28, quest. 5, sect. 2); but there is no reason to linger on the point; for what Scotus thought does not have much relevance to our concerns, especially since his words are particularly equivocal. And in behalf of this opinion *Damascene* is cited, book 3 of *De Fide*, Ch. 11, where he says: "the nature is either to be contemplated in thought alone, or in all hypostases of the same

[70]

species which it conjoins, or only in one individual;" Here by "nature contemplated in thought alone" he means the nature as universal. In this way he says that the universal nature does not exist but is merely to be thought of; however, he says it exists in individuals either in all according to its entire specific amplitude, or in one thing only.

2. This is established by reason since the unity and the disposition to be in many things, insofar as they are necessary elements of the notion of a universal, do not really belong to the nature itself, but accrue to it through the intellect; therefore universality also accrues to it in the same way. This is confirmed and clarified, because, if the nature has universality prior to the operation of intellect, then it has that universality either in itself or in individuals; but it has not this universality in individuals since it neither has it in one alone (because in that thing it is individual and determined to one thing) nor does it have it in many or all alike, since the nature can just as well be universal even if it is found in only one individual; so also, no real property belongs to a nature as existing in many individuals which does not belong to it in singulars or in each of them, with the exception of the multitude of individuations or singularities itself—in which universality does not consist, as is obvious. Also, neither can universality accrue to a nature of itself, prescinding from individuals, except through the intellect since, if such a nature is considered as existing in reality itself, it does not *ex natura rei* prescind from the individuals because it is not *ex natura rei* distinct from them, as has been shown. If, however, the nature is not existing in itself, one cannot conceive which or what kind of status it might have, unless it has that status objectively in the intellect, since it does not really have such status and cannot have it, and besides is not *ex natura rei* distinguished with regard to the being of its essence (or with regard to its possible being) from individuals considered in the same state, as has been often said. Finally, if universal being really belonged to a nature, either it would accrue through the nature itself or by accident; neither can be said; so it does not really belong to the nature; therefore it belongs to the nature merely through the operations of reason. The first part of the minor is obvious, since, if being a universal belonged to "man" through itself, it would also belong to all individuals; for, whatever "of itself primarily" or "of itself secondarily" accrues to the higher, also accrues to the lower (or, what is inferior to the former). And no property can be added to the higher nature on account of the lower[27] where the property would conflict with the essence or the properties belonging to the higher of itself, since these could not be separated from the higher nor could they remain together with conflicting properties. The latter part of the

27 Literally "inferior."

[71]

minor is proved: since, if universality really and contingently or accidentally accrues to the nature, it will be some accident of the nature; then, if it is a real accident it will accrue to it [the nature] by reason of something singular, (as we were arguing above, concerning the unity and the disposition for being in many things). Again, this accident will belong to the nature through some action of an extrinsic agent, or through the lack of such action, if it is imagined to be a privative accident; every action of this kind, however, is essentially related to individuals. Finally, what kind of a real accident this would be, can be neither imagined nor explained; therefore the universality of the nature is a universality of reason and through reason.

3. *The opposing reasons are dissolved*. In reply to the contrary cases set forth in the second section, it has already been declared how the nature in reality is communicable to many things, not through some disposition or indifference which belongs to the nature itself *of itself*, but merely through the non-repugnance of the singular things themselves to having it possible that other things be like them, which non-repugnance is not sufficient for the notion of the universal, as has been declared. Whence, with regard to the first argument, this inference is denied: "Human nature is not of itself incommunicable; therefore of itself it is communicable"; for, speaking strictly it is an inference from a negative to an affirmative on the part of that mode or term "of itself"; and it could happen that neither of these belongs to it *of itself*, although in a thing one of them is always present. But if that particle "of itself" is not taken so strictly that it is the same as "*per se*" and "intrinsically," but is taken only so that "nature by itself" means the same as "the nature from its formal aspect and isolated from every inferior difference," then the inferenec can be conceded rather by reason of the material than by reason of the form. For the nature can be called communicable of itself in the sense explained above because it is not incompatible for it to have several individuals alike in essence and nature among themselves and because it is not incompatible for one individual to have another like it; this non-repugnance is, however, not sufficient for the notion of the universal, as has been said. And the same reply is to be fitted to the second argument; for in the real nature itself there is no positive and real disposition to several individual differences, but there is merely a non-repugnance in these individuals to being able to have other things like them. And it follows from this both that the nature may be called communicable or disposed to be in many things, and that such a nature cannot be adequately contracted through one individual difference, as has been sufficiently explained. To the third argument it is answered that all those attributes express in some way a relation to the intellect; they are grounded in the things

[72]

themselves, not insofar as the nature has any universality in the things, but insofar as there is in the individuals themselves agreement and similarity in essence and its properties and in the intrinsic connection which essence and properties have among themselves by reason of which [intrinsic connections], those common objective concepts are abstracted from which the universal predications of necessary and perpetual truth (insofar as they are abstracted from time) are made. And in this way science is said to be of universals and not of singulars, not because it is concerned with names and not with singulars but because it is concerned with common objective concepts, which, although in reality itself not distinguished from the individuals, are nevertheless distinguished by reason; and that is sufficient ground for all the aforementioned ways of speaking. The nominalists, as we have said, claim this is not enough and indeed speak otherwise, although in reality they do not differ much from us. Through this, a reply is made to the last confirmation. To the other presuppositions nothing further need to be replied, for from what has been said, everyone has been satisfied.

SECTION VI

Through Which Operation of the Intellect Are Things Made Universal?

1. This question put in other words is usually treated in the beginning of dialectics, namely: Whether the universal is produced through abstraction or through comparison of the intellect. It is also usually treated, and more properly, in chapter 3 of *De Anima,* in explaining the object of the understanding, which object is said to be the universal. Although we have said that the universal unity results from the work of the understanding, we cannot pass on without clarifying which and what kind of operation of the intellect this is. It is necessary to briefly distinguish the dual intellect, agent and possible; the work of the former is to produce the intelligible species; the work of the latter is to work with and to understand through those species; it has, however, a double operation (skipping the others which are not relevant to the present matter); the one is called direct, by which it directly inclines to the things which the intelligible species represent and toward which it leads the understanding of itself and simply. The other is called reflex, by which the intellect turns about on prior knowledge or on its object under those conditions or denominations which it receives from knowledge.

2. There can be three opinions on this matter: the first is that the universal is produced through an operation of the agent intellect which precedes every operation of the possible intellect and consists in the production of the intelligible species representing the nature isolated and abstracted from all individuals, which operation is usually called for this reason, the abstraction of the common nature made by virtue of the agent intellect. So, St. Thomas indicates, *Ia*, q.85, a.1, in corpus, and ad 4; and a.2, ad 4; 7 *Metaphysics*, Lect. 13; *De Ente et Ess.* Ch. 4, and *Commentary in 2 de Anima*, Comm. 10: saying: "the intellect is moved to its ultimate perfection by universal things, namely, by the things represented in the intelligible species." And also in 3 *de Anima*, text 8, he says that if the universals were outside the soul, the agent intellect would be useless. Domenic Flanders, 3 *Metaphysics*, q.2, a.2; 7 *Metaphysics*, q.16, a.1; Fonseca, 5 *Metaphysics*, Ch. 28, questions 5 and 6; Soto, in *Logic*, q.3 *On Universals*. This opinion supposes in the first place that the possible intellect does not know material singulars directly and by virtue of the species which it receives from the agent intellect but merely knows the common natures. From this it follows that the species produced by the agent intellect directly represents only the common nature isolated from all individuals, and is consequently "universal in representing." From this it still happens that the nature thus represented becomes objectively and through intrinsic denomination universal through this kind of abstraction; for if the singular and individual is made by contraction, then what is universal and common may be made by abstraction. And this is confirmed since the universal is the object of the agent and possible intellect; of the former, as of an active potency; of the latter, as of a passive or a receptive potency. Therefore, produced through the action of the agent intellect, it precedes the operation of the possible intellect; for it is part of the concept of an active potency that it makes its object; a passive power supposes it; for it usually reacts to it.

3. The second opinion is that the universal is not produced by the agent intellect, but by the possible intellect through a direct operation by which it knows the common nature under its precise formal notion and essence, considering nothing of the inferior aspects or of the individuals, nor even formally, and is it were, *in actu signato*, considering the community of the nature itself, but only the essence which is common. Those who hold that the possible intellect knows singulars and also material things directly, necessarily have to teach this opinion, in particular the earlier negative part in which it differs from the preceding opinion. For according to that opinion it has consequently to be claimed that the agent intellect, speaking *per se*, makes a singular

[74]

species not only "in being" but also "in representing" the individual and singular thing, because the intellect cannot know the thing primarily and directly unless it receives a species which represents it properly and particularly. From this it happens that according to this opinion, the agent intellect does not abstract the universal from singulars and is merely said to abstract the intelligible species from the phantasm because it separates it from the material conditions—with regard to *its real being,* not, however, with regard to the object which it represents; for the intellect produces a species which is spiritual and immaterial, representing the same (in number) individual thing which the phantasm represents; for it is not repugnant that a material individual should be represented intentionally through an immaterial form or quality. And with reference to the universality of the genus, this can be confirmed in all the opinions, since although we might grant that the agent intellect abstracts the *specific* nature from individuals in that manner, it is however not necessary that it abstract the *generic* nature from the species, since it is certain that the possible intellect can be borne directly and immediately to knowing the specific nature and that the agent intellect can produce an intelligible species which does not abstract in its representation from the specific difference, whatever may be the case concerning the individual; therefore that universal which is the genus is not made universal through the abstraction of the agent intellect.

4. The other affirmative part of the opinion, namely, that this universal is sufficiently produced through the abstraction of the possible intellect, can be taken from St. Thomas *Ia,* q.16, a.3, and 2; and *Opusculum* 42, Ch. 5, at the end, where he cites the Commentator, I *De Anima,* text 8: "The intellect produces the universality in things"; which, granted it can be thought to have been said about the agent intellect, will be *a fortiori* true of the possible intellect of which Averroes is speaking; for he is treating the defining and demonstrating intellect. Next, even though the authors cited in the preceding opinion teach that the first universality is produced by the agent intellect, they cannot deny consequently that the operation of the possible intellect may suffice to a like or more perfect universality. And thus, St. Thomas, cited in other places, speaks indifferently of the abstracting intellect, whether agent or possible. Durandus also teaches this more explicitly of the possible intellect alone: I *Sent.,* d.3, q.5, n.27 and in II, d.3, q.7, n.12. And it can be proved *a fortiori* by the reasons for the first opinion, since the concept, or expressed species, of the possible intellect represents more formally than the impressed species; therefore, if the intellect abstractly and in isolation attends minutely to "man", "man" as represented in this concept will be objectively universal much better

than if "man" is represented in the impressed species, because it has a more actual and more proper objective being; and with respect to that being it is universal. And it is confirmed first, for "man" is made singular through individuating differences; therefore by this very fact (that it prescinds through the actual abstract concept from all those differences) it would be made universal. It is confirmed secondly, because if "man" were to exist in reality, just as "man" stands as object to that concept, he would be universal in being, which is the kind of doctrine attributed to Plato; therefore, "man" is also a universal now through denomination by the intellect. It is confirmed thirdly: because, if the intellect reflects upon "man" thus conceived, considering its condition or, as it were, its status, it knows it [man] not to be something singular but to be something common to all singulars, in which conception the intellect does not fail, as is obvious; nor does it even ascribe to "man" thus conceived anything new, but conceives what was previously in a man; therefore, before this reflection, "man" was already universal through a prior direct conception. And a reason put forth for the earlier opinion can also serve for this: that the operation of the intellect supposes an object; for this is true of the object which is known through an operation, not for the condition which results in the object insofar as it is known, when that condition is not known through the same act, since when such a condition results from an act, it is compared to a potency, rather as an active than as a passive potency; so it is in the present case; for universality, which in some way is said to "have being in"[28] or to accrue to a nature known abstractly, is a certain condition or denomination resulting from such an act and mode of knowing; the condition of universality nevertheless, is not known through that act but only the nature itself, which is denominated universal, is known through that act; and hence it is not necessary that the universality of that object be presupposed to that act. But when the intellect afterward reflects upon and contemplates that very condition or state of the abstract nature, the condition is already an object known through such an act; therefore it is supposed to that act, and nevertheless that condition is nothing other than the universality of the nature; therefore universality is presupposed to this reflexive or (what it is the same) comparative notion; it is produced, however, through the abstractive or through (what it is the same) direct and precise knowledge of the universal nature.

5. The third opinion is that the universal is made through a comparative cognition by which the possible intellect, after it apprehends the nature precisely and abstractly, compares it as thus conceived, with the things in which it exists, and understands it as one thing dis-

---

[28] Latin: *"inesse."*

posed to be in many inferiors and to be predicated of them. And so according to this opinion, the nature existing in singulars has universality only in *remote potency*, since it is neither common positively, (like something truly one but existing in many things) nor even negatively (like something proper to no single thing). But there is in it only a certain similarity and agreement of several things among themselves which furnishes the occasional and remote basis of universality. The nature known abstractly can be called universal in proximate potency because it is already negatively common, since it is conceived by itself and not as proper to any individual; however, it is not yet to be thought to be actually universal, since it is not yet conceived as having the disposition and relation to the many things in which it is; it receives that relation [predicability of many] through a comparative cognition and hence through it, [comparative cognition] it is said to be finally constituted a universal in act.

This is further proved because universality is not any thing having true existence, but is only a being or relation of reason; therefore it has only objective being in the intellect; therefore it only exists when it is actually made by the intellect, for then only is it objectively in the intellect; therefore it exists only through comparative cognition since through it alone is it made or excogitated by the intellect.

This is supported, for the universal as universal is relative as is obvious, *both* from its definition; for it is defined through its correlative, namely: "It is one in many and of many"; *and* from its species, namely, "genus," "species," "difference," etc.; for these are spoken of relatively, as is obvious from the definitions given by Porphyry in the predicables. However, relative things are simultaneous in nature and in cognition; therefore, the universal in act does not exist in that manner in which it *can* be, namely, objectively in the intellect, until its correlative exists in the same way; it cannot however be in that way until one thing is compared to another, which happens only through the said comparative cognition; therefore . . . [the universal is produced through comparative cognition and through comparative cognition the nature is finally constituted a universal.] And St. Thomas favors this opinion, and teaches everywhere that relations of reason only exist in the apprehension of reason comparing one thing to another: *Ia*, q.2 both in a.1, corpus, and ad 4; and q.7, *De Potentia*, a.1; and 4 *Metaphysics*, Lect 4; and Book I of *De Interpretatione*, Lect 10. Also Cajetan means this, when he treats generally of the relation of reason, in the mentioned question 28, first part, and in particular of the relation of universaliy, in *Being and Essence*, Ch. 4, q.7, and a little before that. Also Scotus, 7 *Metaphysics*, q.11; Anthony Andreas q.17; and Anthony Trombeta, in 2 *Metaphysics* first article—are all cited; for the way in

[77]

which they suppose the universal to be in act through the intellect, seems to be a comparative cognition rather than in an isolating cognition. There is, however, a difference among those authors, that some of them mean by "comparative cognition" a direct knowledge by which the universal is compared with its inferiors as it exists in them or is predicable of them. St. Thomas seems to think thus and Scotus more clearly so, as cited above, and also in IV, d.2; Soncinas, 6 *Met.* q.18. Others mean a reflexive knowledge in which, after the aforementioned comparison the intellect conceives the comparison itself as a certain relation and comparative nature, as a genus or a species, etc. with respect to the inferiors.

A Judgment Is Passed Upon the First Opinion

6. Among these opinions, the first is indeed probable from the supposition of that opinion that the agent intellect does not produce species representing individuals and thus far (supposing that), it does not deal generally with every universal but chiefly with the specific, and with it alone formally speaking—as a little thought on what has been done, proves. And it can be further clarified since it is especially certain that the agent intellect never impresses a species representing only the difference, as it is a difference, but rather species representing the whole specific nature. Just as the phantasm does not represent anything in the individual through the mode of a form, but only through the mode of a whole individual, so the agent intellect produces a species representing the whole specific nature of the individual in the manner of a whole, nor can it prescind from or alter that action so that it could then produce one species representing the difference through the mode of a form, until it should produce another, representing the entire specific nature in the manner of a whole; but it is not free in acting but naturally impresses the species, as far as it can, given such and such a phantasm; nor is it cognoscitive so that it can now conceive the nature in one manner and afterward in another. Whence, this holds both in the case of "property" and also in the case of "accident," although we grant that it produces species representing them in common by abstracting from the individuals; nevertheless each of them is alone represented by virtue of such an intelligible species as something common to many individuals alike in that respect. And the same thing is true in its own way on the generic level, if by chance an intelligible species representing only this level is produced because of the debility of the phantasm; for, just as the phantasm represents this one thing as animal, for example, so the intelligible species taken from it will represent the level "animal" only, as abstracted and isolated from similar individuals. And for that reason we say that, even supposing the truth of that opinion, nothing but the specific na-

ture is abstracted through this abstraction of the agent intellect by itself. You may object that this move can be made concerning the abstraction made through the conception of the possible intellect, especially in regard to the universal of "property" and "accident." I reply that there is no parallel at all, as will appear from what we will say in the following section.

7. Therefore I add further that if the notion and nature of the intelligible species be properly and truly understood, it will be quite improper to say that the nature is made universal through this abstraction since, according to the true opinion, the impressed species is neither a formal image nor does it in any way formally represent, but rather represents effectively, only inasfar as it is, as it were, the seed or instrument of the object in producing the formal intentional representation which occurs through the conception of the mind.[29] Whence, the nature is not properly said to be objectively represented in the impressed species, except remotely and mediately indeed, inasfar as that species is effective of the act to which that nature stands as object. And next, even if we grant that the universal is produced in some way through the abstraction of the agent intellect, it will be only in disposition or in "first act"; from this, it happens that it is much more, and more perfectly, produced through the second act related to that first act, as we were arguing above. I omit the fact that the first opinion proceeds from a false hypothesis; for it is simply more likely that the impressed species is *not* abstracted by the agent intellect from a representation of the same individual represented in the phantasm, but is abstracted only from the real and entitative materiality of that phantasm, without which[30] it could be a representation of this same individual, although material; for it is not repugnant for it to be or become this through a form or a quality or a spiritual entity, as is clear in the case of the angels and in the case of God, himself. If it is not absurd, then no physical reason can be put forward on account of which such

[29] When Suarez says the impressed species is merely an *effective* representation of the thing conceived and not a formal (or structural) representation, he is proposing a quite new and revolutionary doctrine about the impressed species and the function of the agent intellect. He says, in sum, that the function of the agent intellect is solely dematerialization and (since he does not maintain that individuation is a result of materiality), he disagrees with Aquinas by denying that universalization results from dematerialization of the species. Suarez discusses this point extensively and eruditely in his *De Anima*, Book IV, Chapter 3 and in Book III, Chapter 2, Number 20, where he says "Intentional species do not represent their objects formally, but only effectively." See also note 13, p. 46 above.

[30] "Without which [abstraction], it [the phantasm] could be . . . etc." This seems to be the most plausible interpretation of the statement, although others are possible.

[79]

a form or species cannot be produced by the agent intellect; this is not to be denied without reason, since this is more consonant, both with various experiments and with the natural order of knowing, and with the end and the natural activity of the agent intellect, which is given as a medium for this and renders the possible intellect (by a spiritual act) like the representation in the phantasm, insofar as it can; this is something which it would be foreign to the present matter to follow up and prove more extensively. According to that opinion [the first of the three] it is obvious that the abstraction of the universal in no way happens necessarily by the agent intellect; indeed, in no way at all can it happen; for if the agent intellect be supposed to be producttive of the species of singular things, it is very likely that it can never produce species representing natures abstracted from singulars; but, more of that in its proper place.

The Other Two Opinions Are Examined and the Question Is Decided

8. Therefore skipping the first opinion, so as to judge the other two, it must be noticed that we can conceive or denominate the universal in two ways. First, it can be conceived as something absolute with regard to its being, which can be the basis for some relation. Secondly, as relative in being, bespeaking an order to inferiors. In the first sense one would mean a universal substance, if there were a man in reality subsisting separately from every contraction, according to the Platonic opinion; nor would it be a universal because of a real relation in being to inferiors, but because of its unity along with an intrinsic and substantial disposition toward existing in many things. The writers cited in the preceeding section were saying, in almost this sense, that a nature in the potential state which it is imagined to have before its existence in individuals has a certain universality which does not consist in a relation of being, but in a certain absolute property of a nature having such unity and community; this used to be called by some, the *universal ante rem;* which if it should exist, would be absolute; nevertheless there is really no such universal. More, even those who suppose the universal-in-act to be really existing in the individuals themselves (which is called the *universal in re*) do not posit its universality in a relation. For they think universality is real and not in the least a relation, *either* since there is not a sufficient distinction in reality between the nature and the individual for a real distinction; *or* since the nature as it prescinds from individuals, does not have enough entity to support a real relation because it does not have the singular being in which it would be possible to base such a relation. Therefore they place this universality in an absolute property which is some kind of unity and community belonging to such a nature. These examples, although not

[80]

true, make clear, nevertheless, that the universal concept as such is not the concept of a thing relative in being, but of an absolute thing having that kind of being which affords indifference and a disposition for being in many things. Nor does the view take notice of the fact that this aptitude might seem to be explained in the manner of a relation. For, just as we understand in the case of a real potency that the transcendental relation and the relation regarded by language is prior to the predicamental relation in being and is included in absolute reality, so in the present case we can conceive this disposition of the universal thing as absolute in itself, even though it is explained through the mode of a transcendental relation. And hence it happens further that this disposition, since it is conceived in the manner of a potency having at least a transcendental relation to those things to which it can communicate itself, can also be understood as the sufficient basis for the relation or disposition toward those things to which it can communicate itself, which disposition is conceived as a certain relation in being; it can also be said to be a certain kind of universality, because it is the disposition of one thing to the many things in which it can have being or of which it can be predicated.

9. Therefore, the universal conceived in the first manner is produced through the direct operation of the understanding which precisely and abstractly conceives the common nature apart from contracting differences; the reasons produced for the second opinion sufficiently prove this. And it can be confirmed by our destroying the basis of the third opinion; because there is not any relation in being involved in the notion of the universal; therefore, although there is not understood to be any relation in being toward inferiors in the nature thus abstracted, it can still be understood to be actually universal. What follows is obvious, since, if that relation is not necessary, nothing else can be lacking, since here is the common nature *and* in the manner of something subsisting abstractly from individuals. Whence, as it stands in this state through the intellect, so it would stand really, if in reality it subsisted outside individuals; but then it would be really universal; therefore it is also now intentionally universal, as I say. Yet in a nature thus conceived there is a new unity of reason since it has one objective concept, indivisible into several similar ones; it also has a community or aptitude to be in many things and to be predicated of them; therefore nothing is lacking to the notion "universal."

10. But speaking of the relation of universality insofar as it is conceived by us in the manner of a relation of being,—this cannot result through abstraction alone, but it happens to be, in the way in which it exists, through a comparison, since, as I suppose, the relation is not real but one of reason; therefore it does not exist in the nature itself

[81]

while it is thought of absolutely and abstractly, since it is not, by virtue of that action, represented through the intellect, because the intellect has not yet compared it to its inferiors, nor is it represented really, either; therefore there is not yet any such relation. And the reasons alledged for the third opinion prove this well enough. Concerning this, if two opinions affirm the one thing and do not exclude the other, then they are not mutually contrary, nor do the reasons for one weigh against the other. Nothing prohibits the possibility that a double relation of universality accrues to the same nature through the intellect, namely: absolute and relative; and that those relations should be created through different operations of the understanding, and that the one, which is absolute, should be the proximate basis for the other, namely, the relative. Nor does it seem absurd that something should belong to a nature through the intellect and should have being in the manner of an absolute, when it is of the kind that accrues only through extrinsic denomination; for, the nature's being abstracted or universally conceived adds nothing to the nature, except a certain being [esse] belonging to it through extrinsic denomination, which being is called "objective being."[31] Just as to be seen and to be known is not any real being [esse] added to things, nor does it consist formally in a relation of reason, but it rather consists in a denomination arising from the act of seeing or knowing, upon which the intellect can construct a relation of reason if it compares one thing with the other; so it is in the present matter.

11. But now there is left to be explained, concerning these opinions, what kind of knowledge, isolating or comparative, it is through which the mentioned universal is produced in each of the mentioned ways. For the universal nature can be isolated or compared in various ways. First, the common nature can be abstracted through a pure isolation of the nature from every inferior without any comparison either of the higher concept to the same inferior or any comparison of the inferiors among themselves, as when the common nature is abstracted from Peter alone, simply ignoring the individuating properties, and sticking with a consideration of human nature. And some think that no universal is produced through this purely isolating knowledge. It is more likely that through this knowledge the absolute universal is made in accordance with those things we said of the second opinion. For the reasons put forth also prove this, although this knowledge does not suffice for the apprehension [in the nature thus concerned] of the universality or superiority which it has, as I shall soon say.

12. Secondly, the common nature can be abstracted through the comparison of singulars or inferiors, as when by comparing Peter with

31 Or "to be objectively."

[82]

Paul, I know them to be alike in human nature. This comparison supposes a prior isolation, for it supposes that one knows of each singular that it is of such and such a nature; whence it supposes a concept of such a nature in order for it to be isolated from the single individuals. Whence, only the agreement and similarity of several inferiors in such an abstracted and isolated nature is knowledge added through this comparison. This comparison can be further subdistinguished, insofar as there can be considered through it, either (a): only the disposition of particulars among themselves to having among themselves the relation of similars, and this comparison as such does not pertain to the constitution of the universal but to a consideration of some mutual relation among the particulars. Or (b): insofar as the disposition of the common nature toward the particulars in which it exists is considered. For after the intellect apprehends Peter and Paul to be similar in their being men, it again notices that this predicate "man" is related to Peter and Paul as something common to particulars; and in this comparison the notion of the universal seems to be completed, even the notion of the respective universal;[32] for there arises in the mind through this comparison, or rather in the reality standing as object to the mind, a relation of reason of one thing being common to many. Further, the other knowledge can be understood as more reflexive than the intellect produces by knowing the nature thus abstracted, and related to its inferiors, as it were *in actu signato*, and knowing it to have the denominations of genus, species and the like; and these denominations are of reason not of reality. Indeed this knowledge is not the construction of universality but is a certain more formal and express contemplation of it.

SECTION VII

Whether the Universals Are Real Beings, Corporeal, Substantial or Accidental, and What Causes They Have

1. From what has been said various questions which are usually treated concerning universals can be quickly settled.
FIRST DOUBT IS SETTLED

2. It is first asked whether universals are entities or not. The question can be asked either about the nature which is denominated universal or about that intention or denomination of universality. Concerning the nature, we have already said that it exists in the things

---

[32] That is, he means that the logical pre-requisites for being-a-universal area fulfilled, even those for being a "respective universal."

[83]

themselves; whence it happens that with regard to the thing denominated, universals are real entities; this is to be understood either permissively or of these universals which of themselves fall under the direct operation of the intellect so that they can be either directly known by themselves or at least through the direct knowing of their proper singulars. Moreover this is said because in the very entities of reason which are constructed through the reflection and multiplex operation of the intellect, the intellect can advance so that from these it may also abstract universal and common notions and also put together the universal on fictitious matters which are not true entities, in the manner in which the dialectitions say that a genus taken second-intentionally is a certain specific universal, common to many genera which differ only in number with regard to the notion or intention of genus; and thus of the others. The reason is that the universal in act has only objective being in the intellect; however, objective being in the intellect can belong not only to true beings but also to fictions; and therefore one can also attribute to them those relations or denominations which merely require this kind of being, for example: the notions "subject" and "predicate"; it is the same with the notion "universal." And hence we say that universals are permissively or indefinitely real entities, not, however, necessarily and entirely universally. The cognition of the intellect begins necessarily from real things, both because a reflex operation presupposes a direct operation, and also because fictitious entities are not conceived unless through some relation or proportion to true entities; hence it is rightly said that those universals are real beings which can be abstracted through a direct operation of the understanding. If, however, the discussion turns on universality itself, or on the intention of universality, the common universality is said not to be a real being but to be a being of reason, which is true in this sense, namely, that it is not some property, or something intrinsically and really inherent in the nature which is denominated universal, according to what we have said. Yet, in another sense there is need for some distinction and clarification. For we say in two senses that a nature can be denominated universal; first, by an absolute denomination, as if it were subsisting universally; secondly, by a relative denomination. In the first sense, universality is not a being of reason as something properly constructed by reason, but only as an extrinsic denomination arising from an act of reason, like "being abstracted," "being known," and other things of this kind which do not imply something existing really in the denominated nature and do not properly imply any being of reason fabricated by the intellect as though it were something objectively constructed by it, because such entities are not constructed except while they are being thought of; then, however, the

[84]

intellect thinks or knows no such thing. Therefore, it is an extrinsic denomination from the concept of the intellect; they are represented abstractly and universally through a concept, therefore they are denominated universal in the aforesaid way. For this reason it is not necessary, in order for this universality to be said to have being, that it be known formally and reflexively, as it were in *actu signato*, but it is sufficient that the nature itself be known in such a manner, (namely: precisely and abstractly) in order that the nature be constituted universal, as it were, *in actu exercito*. Soto explains universality through extrinsic denomination in this manner in *Logica* q.3, *Univer.*, art. 1, d.2; and he cites Scotus and St. Thomas as being of this opinion.

3. Speaking, in the latter sense, of the universal relatively, or of the relation of universality, it is sufficiently established from what has been said that the universal is not a real being, since that relation is not real but of reason. This is clarified briefly in the following way. For a multiple relation can be thought of or imagined in the universal nature: one in relation to the act of being; another in relation to the act of predicating; either can, however, be apprehended as a disposition or as an act; for the common nature is conceived as disposed to have existence in many things, and as such it can be conceived as having the relation or disposition to communicating itself to those things; again it can be conceived as actually existing in those things, and as such, having an actual relation or the relation of a thing in-act-communicating itself to many things. For just as we make part of our understanding of an accident the relation of "disposition" or of actual inhesion, so we can imagine or think of it in the universal nature as communicable or as communicated to many things. And the universal is usually defined in both ways; yet the relation of aptitude [disposition] suffices, for the nature to be thought completely universal. For, what actually has being in many things which exist is contingent, and does not change the nature of the thing; a disposition is indeed simply necessary, for in it the universal is distinguished from the singular. Whence they who say that the angelic natures are universal and are incommunicable to many things are involved in absurdity.

4. Similarly, the nature can be conceived in relation to the act of predicating, either as disposed to be predicated of many things or as actually predicated of many things; the former consideration properly denominates the nature "predicable." However, all those relations are merely of reason; for the universal nature is not in many things except through identity and thence under that aspect it cannot be really related to the many things. Again, as we have said, there is in reality no nature which is in many or which is disposed to be in many; therefore the proximate basis of those relations is not in reality, but is in

[85]

the manner of the intellect's conceiving; so a relation founded in it cannot be real; and this reason clearly proves the same thing for the relation of "predicate" or "the predicated," for all of these are also grounded in the extrinsic denominations of the intellect, and hence cannot be real.

THE SECOND DOUBT IS DISPELLED

5. *Whether universals are corporeal or not.* And immediately after these things another question must be clarified, one which Porphyry proposed concerning the predicables, namely, whether universals are corporeal. For in the same way, it must be said that it is indeed possible that some universals are corporeal, those doubtless, which belong to things composed of matter and form, as is obvious from the concept of man, of horse, of animal, of body; moreover these universals are especially well accommodated to the human intellect conjoined to a body; for it receives its knowledge from sensible things, and therefore conceives and abstracts these universals first, strictly speaking. Yet absolutely speaking, the notion of a universal is not limited to corporeal natures; for it is found in spiritual natures; among them are also found singular things having the mutual agreement and difference or distinction by reason of which common and universal natures can be conceived in them. Indeed, not only the spiritual things have mutual agreement and disagreement, and the corporeal things mutual agreement and difference, but also the corporeal things have some agreement and likeness to spiritual things; therefore, not only are some universals corporeal and others incorporeal, but some universals are also found to be common to both, like "substance," "quality," etc. For these abstract from whether things are corporeal or incorporeal.

A THIRD DIFFICULTY

6. *Whether universals are substances or accidents.* Whence the similar question of whether universals are substances or accidents is easily dispelled. For this question, like the preceding one, is not properly concerned with the notion of "universal"; for that, since it is not anything real but merely a denomination or relation of reason, is neither truly a substance nor an accident, neither a body nor a spirit, although it must be conceived in the manner of an incorporeal accident. The aforesaid question is therefore concerned with the nature which is denominated universal; and this can be not only substantial but also accidental, as is intrinsically obvious. It is true that Aristotle was given to say that universals are not substances; as 3 *Metaphysics,* text 20; Book 6, text 45; he meant, however, that they are not things subsisting through and of themselves outside singulars. And so in the *Predicaments,* in the chapter on substances, he calls substantial uni-

[86]

versals "second substances"; he calls the individuals of the substances, or the supposits, "first substances," which he says are more substances than the second substances, because the former subsist first, the others subsist in them.

The Fourth Difficulty

7. *Those which are called eternal universals—an objection is resisted.* Another question about universals is settled from what has been said, namely, whether they are eternal. For they are commonly thought to be, because, given that they are the proper objects of the sciences, they must be necessary and immutable and consequently eternal. However, how this is to be understood is not explained by everyone in the same way. Plato for this reason posited ideas which are eternal and immutable forms, as Aristotle interprets him. Aristotle himself would perhaps say that the universals in these corruptible things are eternal, since these are never lacking some of those singulars in which they exist. We, however, assume that these singulars do not always exist and that outside them there do not exist universals: whence we conclude that these cannot be called eternal with regard to the real existence which they have beyond their causes. Therefore these universals are called perpetual, with regard to the being of the essence or potential being. You must say: individuals are also eternal in this way since they are also eternally possible, and they have immutable essences with regard to the being of the essence. Whence, there can be produced propositions about them which have perpetual truth, insofar as they are abstracted from time. It is replied that with respect to the reality it is indeed thus, yet there is a difference in the manner of conceiving and speaking; for universals as such, by the fact that they are abstracted from singulars, are consequently separated also from time and place and from every change, beginning and cessation, and thus St. Thomas says correctly (*Ia*, q.16, a.7, ad 2) "Universals are usually said to be everywhere and always, not positively but negatively," that is, not because they are in every place and every time, but because they do not as such determine for themselves a time and a place, insofar as they are abstracted from here and now. This, however, does not properly belong to individuals; for actions, and changes, beginnings and cessations concern them. Whence, although some universals are generable and corruptible, like "man," "animal," and the like, which from their formal notion bear along with themselves such a potency or postulate such a manner of beginning and cessation, yet they do not have this property except in relation to individuals; for "man," as such, can neither be generated nor corrupted, and yet is *called* generable and corruptible since it is of such a nature that it cannot be communicated in its connatural manner to individuals except through generation and that very

individual which shares such a nature is of itself a subject of corruption. Some also add that universals are eternal because a unity of isolation and a disposition for being in many things belongs to them perpetually, even when they do not exist, in the same way in which the other properties are said to belong to them perpetually, by separating the copula from the existence of time. Thus Fonseca, Book 5, Ch. 28, q.8, sect. 3. But I do not see how this could be true, unless we admit that some universality belongs to the nature of itself and necessarily; for the proposition which is called a perpetual truth, must be necessary from the connection of the terms, it cannot, however, be thus necessary unless it exist of itself in some way; and hence I do not think universals can be called eternal in this sense, except in relation to some intellect which is eternal, as St. Thomas expressly said in the mentioned solution to the second objection.

THE FIFTH DIFFICULTY

8. *Whether there are causes of the universals or not.* The last question can be understood from the words: whether and how universals have causes; for the discussion is concerned either with universal natures or with their universality. In the former sense, just as the universal natures do not happen except in individuals, so they do not have causes except in them, nor do they have them otherwise, for they are both made by the same efficient agent and they arise (if they are composite) from the same principles or from the same matter and form, and they are ordained by the nature itself to the same end. If we are talking of the universality itself, since it is not a real being, it is not necessary for it to have proper and real causes; yet, in the same way as it is a being or rather imitates being, it has in its own way a material and an efficient cause; for that nature which is denominated universal imitates a material cause insofar as it is like a subject which undergoes the intention of universality, and is denominated universal because of it; since universality is not a real intrinsic form, then it [the nature] is not the subject of inherence but of denomination, and it is more the material "about which" than the material "in which" or "out of which." The intellect which makes the concept representing that nature abstractly (or makes the comparison of the nature thus abstracted with its inferiors), is itself the efficient cause; for properly speaking it does not make the relation of reason but considers it or imagines it not so much in *actu signato* as in *actu exercito*, as I have said, by conceiving the disposition as if it were a true relation. It is not necessary to seek a formal and final cause here, for the very universality of the universal itself, thus actually considered, is like a form which is nothing other than either the denomination arising from the act of the intellect, or the relation of reason founded and conceived in it. The end of this

[88]

universality either is nothing, properly speaking, since the universality is only something resulting from the conception of the intellect intending knowledge of things; or, if some end must be assigned, it is only the very same knowledge of the intellect, because by considering the essences of things it abstracts their formal levels and relations; and since it has the power of perceiving and discerning everything and of reflecting upon its own actions themselves, it not only intends to know the natures of things, but also the denominations or appearances which they seem to have insofar as they stand as objects to that same intellect and for this end it constructs universals and structures their relations.

SECTION VIII

How Many is the Universal, or Its Unity

1. We have explained what kind may be the unity of the universal and in what way the universal belongs in things; it remains for us to make clear the various modes of this unity or universality, so that from here it may be obvious what difference there may be in this matter between the metaphysical and dialectical universal and for what reason the universals must be distinguished from one another or multiplied.

FIRST DIVISION

2. *What the universal "in causing" is—What it is "in representing."* The universal is usually divided into the *universal in causing*, the *universal in representing*, the *universal in being*, and the *universal in predicating*. But this division, with regard to the two first members, is not relevant to the present matter. For a cause is called universal because it can produce various effects in some singular thing, such as God, the heavens, etc.; whence it does not have any other unity except real singular or numerical unity; but it is spoken of as, as it were, universal-in-object since its power is extended to several effects just as the intellect and the will are ordinarily called "objectively universal powers," since they are concerned with all entities, and common sense can also be called universal in the same sense, with respect to external things, although it is one and singular in itself. And the same must be said of the "universal in signifying" or "representing," whether that refers to the names which are called "common terms" by the dialecticians, or to intelligible species, or to formal concepts or, finally, to some image supposed for some reason as uniformly representing several things; for whatever represents in this way is one simple individual in itself and is called universal only on the part of its object, because it signifies or represents several things. However, the third kind of universal,

[89]

which is called the *universal in being* is either nothing at all, or it coincides with the fourth in reality and differs only in name and relation of the reason. For, if "universal in being" refers to that which is universal in the things itself, then there is no universal of this sort, as we have explained; however, if it be that which has its basis in reality yet is conceived through the intellect as something existing in many and as thus *made* universal in being, then this is "universal in predicating"; for it can be predicated of many since it is in them through some identity, as we have explained. But is it properly called a universal by reason of the prior disposition in relation to being, and it is called predicable by reason of the secondary disposition in relation to predication. Whence the dialecticians usually say that "being predicable" is like a property or a passion of the universal.

THE SECOND DIVISION

3. *What is the metaphysical universal—What is the physical universal.* Secondly, the universal is customarily divided into the metaphysical universal, the physical universal, and the logical universal, which can be called, in other words, the universal *ante rem, in re,* and *post rem.* A universal would be most properly called metaphysical if it existed in reality separated from individuals; for in reality it would be abstracted from any change and contraction: the metaphysician especially, considers things thus abstracted. And hence Aristotle, in the books of the *Metaphysics,* especially Book 7, inquires particularly about this universal and shows that there is really none, but that this metaphysical universal is to be distinguished from the others only by reason. Again, the nature itself inasfar as it exists in individuals can be called the "physical universal" and in this sense, the universal is not considered formally, as it is universal, but only materially, in place of the nature which can be abstracted and denominated universal. This universal is called physical because when it is contracted in the singular things themselves it is subject to change and to the sensible accidents from which physical consideration begins. However, this universal is not beyond metaphysical consideration both because it can be found in immaterial things and things abstracting from their being in matter, and also because this universal requires some formal unity, the consideration of which pertains to the metaphysician. Moreover, even the dialectician considers this universal in some way, not *per se* because of the natures thus universal, but only insofar as it is the remote basis and, as it were, the subject of the intention of universality.

4. *What is the logical universal?* That universal in act which arises through the operation of the intellect is entitled the "logical universal"; for since it is the task of the dialectician to treat the operations of the intellect in connection with properly and correctly constructing defini-

[90]

tions, divisions, and arguments, which are chiefly concerned with things conceived universally and mutually compared and coordinated, it is hence necessary that he consider the intentions of reason or the denominations arising thence, although this is not so proper to the dialecticians that it cannot more properly pertain to the metaphysician and also pertain in some way to the physicist. For when he is disputing on the soul, he consequently treats the intellect and its acts and its object; both because it is in some way the proper object of the intellect, and also because it arises through abstraction or comparison, which are proper operations of the intellect. However, this especially pertains to the metaphysician, for as we saw above, it is his business to distinguish the beings of reason from the real beings and to explain what essence and entity they have—something which is especially alien to the task of the dialectician; but he does touch these things obliquely, in order to order the work of the intellect and direct it to a reliable method and art. If we wish to attribute to each what is proper, the metaphysician considers the proper notion of the universal. insofar as it is one in many, and whatever accrues to it by reason of the fact that it presents the nature of the being and the essence and its properties. The dialectician only considers the notion of what is predicable, *per se,* not considering its quiddity or entity but only what one must know in order to build definitions or predications. It is appropriate to the present matter and to the convenient use of the terms that we should call every universal in act (under the aspect of universal) a metaphysical universal; under the aspect of the predicable, it should be called a dialectical [logical] universal.

THIRD DIVISION INTO FIVE UNIVERSALS

5. Thirdly, and something which especially pertains to the matter at hand, the universal is customarily divided into the five branches which Porphyry distinguished in discussing the predicables, namely genus, species, difference, property, and accident. I have no intention of disputing about the quality and sufficiency of this division; for it cannot be done appropriately without exact knowledge of the separate predicables; however, to talk about the separate predicables is foreign to our task; we hope, however, with God's help, to treat each in its proper place. Concerning the distinction we gave above of the universal concept in the manner of an absolute, we need only to recall how it arises through the simple abstractive or isolating conception of the intellect, and from the universal's having been related or compared to its inferiors. Therefore it can be inquired in what way this division must be understood, concerning which universal or the universal conceived under which aspect, namely: absolute or relative, or metaphysical or logical. There can be two ways of replying. The first is that the

[91]

logical universal (and not the metaphysical universal, or the universal as precisely abstracted) is here divided as it is related to reason. For in the case of the metaphysical universal as such, it does not seem possible that those five branches can be always and entirely distinguished appropriately. For, although they are sometimes easily distinguished in diverse natures or concepts, as in "man," "animal," etc., nevertheless, they cannot be distinguished in others, if we stick with an absolute concept, until a relation or comparison to different things is produced. Thus "white," for example, abstractly conceived is a certain universal; it cannot be called a predicable accident rather than a species, as it appears in that abstraction, because it is capable of both relationships with respect to different things; whence until a comparison to different things is made, that double aspect cannot be distinguished in it. Something similar can be considered concerning "property" which can have, with respect to different things the aspect of property and that of species; moreover, the generic nature, even though it may be substantial, and although the genus is denominated with respect to the species, yet with respect to the *individual* properties (according to the probable opinion of many) has the aspect of species.[33] Why should it not also be probable that "difference," although constituting a universal property with respect to the species or the individuals, yet with respect to the inferiors of the differences taken formally, should constitute another aspect of predication or be recalled to the predicable of *species;* for example, "rational" is predicated of this rational being, taken formally, not *in quale* but *in quid,* something which it is not proper to discuss and examine further here.[34] Therefore only the ultimate species of a substantial or accidental nature, taken in the abstract, is entirely incapable of another relation as a universal and does not have other inferiors to which it can be compared besides the individuals whose whole quiddity it contains. Therefore that division does not seem to have a place with respect to the universal insofar as it arises precisely through abstraction.

6. But if you should inquire what kind of name that universal must be given, it can be answered that the notion of the universal under this aspect consists only in the isolating[35] [praecisiva] separation from singulars from which arises a certain unity of reason with a disposition toward many things; this disposition is (under this isolating considera-

[33] An example might be: *"Animality's being here,"* where "being here" is an individual property and 'animality' which usually names a genus here gives the species to which the individual proprety "being here" belongs.

[34] All statements of *in quid* predication are analytic or self-contradictory. Most statements of *in quale* predication are synthetic.

[35] Literally: "precisive" from the Latin: *"praecisiva."*

[92]

tion of its notion) in each universal. And hence, "universal" as such is not further divided but retains merely the nature of "universal" until it is compared with inferiors and receives various denominations with relation to different things. And thus, under this aspect, the universal is not compared to the aforementioned branches, like a genus to differences, but rather as a subject to accidents or as a proximate foundation to the various relations by which it can be denominated. Whence, when the dialecticians make it customary that "universal" or "predicable genus" be applied to the five universals or predicables, the application must be understood formally and with due allowances, as something conceived *relatively* in common.

7. *The sufficing of five predicables.* If one considers the universal as it is compared to the inferiors, it is rightly divided into these five branches; the reason for this division can thus be briefly assigned. For what is one in many, or predicable of many, can be said to be something essential to them or something outside the essence; further, if it be essential, it either expresses the whole essence and is thus the specific universal which can only be common to individuals differing in number since only individuals of this kind can agree in their entire essence; or it expresses *part* of the essence, and this can happen in two ways. First, it might be like something *material* and potential, and thus the universal "genus" is constituted which, as such, is necessarily related to the different species, since that agreement in generic nature (which is the basis of this universality) is neither in the total essence of the thing nor in what is its ultimate formal constituent and determinant, but is in a certain potential level, determinable through several differences.

Secondly it can happen that the universal expresses part of the essence in the manner of a *form* constituting its formal unity, and thus the universal "difference" is constituted and is said to be predicated *in quale quid*[36] because it behaves in the manner of a form constituting the quiddity. This manner of universality and of predication can sometimes be common to things differing in species and sometimes to things differing only in number, as occurs with the ultimate and subalternate differences. And the reason is that such a manner of constitution, though an essential difference of itself, neither excludes further differences essentially constituting and distinguishing specific essences, nor requires them; whence, because this is accidental *to* such a universal, it also happens accidentally to it that the inferiors in which it is found differ in number and species. However, how these things are to be reconciled with what Porphyry taught in his chapter *On Difference,*

---

[36] That is, it is predicated in the manner of something which indicates *what kind of quiddity* is under discussion.

[93]

and what he thought about this, must be left to the logical commentaries. Next, if the universal or predicable be outside the essence, it can be either *per se* connected with the essence and flowing from it; and this is called "property." If it is not connected *per se* with the essence but is contingent and belongs entirely accidentally, it is called "accident," the fifth predicable.

8. Although property and accident, as well, are forms of those things of which they are predicated, still they must not be taken in the abstract, but in the concrete in order to be able to take on the aspect of such universals, since in the other sense, they are not appropriately attributed to their inferiors in such a manner. Rather if such forms are conceived in the abstract, they do not regard their subjects in that manner in which a universal regards its inferiors, but in the manner in which an act regards the potency which it can inform; therefore in order for them to be compared to such inferiors under such a relation and under the aspect of universals, they must be conceived in the concrete, in the manner of a common whole which is in the inferiors subject to it and can be correctly predicated of them. This is a fact which can be observed in all universals also; for it is true in all, that the concrete can alone be predicated of the concrete, and consequently only with respect to them can it have the relation of universal. For this reason it is usually said that a universal is not related to or predicated of its inferiors except in the manner of a whole; for, although we may say that genus and difference do not formally express the whole essence but only the metaphysical part, yet for them to have the relation of universals it is necessary that they be conceived in the manner of a whole, and hence they must be understood *both* in the concrete, as at least implicitly expressing the whole thing, *and* at least in potency including many inferiors, in the way Porphyry said the genus is the whole (namely potential) with respect to the species; and Aristotle in I *Physics*, Ch. 1, says the universal is a certain kind of whole. We shall touch upon how abstract substantivals share the notion of "universal" and how the predication of the universal has point with regard to them, in section 10 of this disputation.

9. *Several objections arise.*—Various objections which are customarily made against the sufficiency of this division as thus explained, and which are the business of the dialecticians, usually arise at this point; and hence, I merely mention that this division can on two grounds be thought not to be properly handled. First, because in it all the ultimate concepts of universals are not enumerated, since "difference" can be divided into several, and likewise "property," etc. Or, if these are said to embrace all under the general notions of difference and property, it will seem an otherwise inept and superfluous division

since it can be reduced to fewer general members; for "genus" and "species" do not seem to agree actually any less than "general" and "special difference."

10. *Why difference is contained in one predicable.* But this difficulty is of no importance, because whether those members are ultimate and specific or merely general, it will be nonetheless a sufficient division, at least on this head: because no other member is brought forward which is not contained under the ones given. And although we grant that some members are general and some specific, it will not be on that account an inept division; for it is not necessary that the members of a division be equal or equally abstract and common; it suffices that they be contained under what is divided and be in some way opposed, and that they exhaust what is divided. It is accidental that some are listed under a more common and others under a less common notion; and on account of peculiar causes, (as, perhaps, has happened in the present case) it is sometimes advantageous, since the distinction of those five members was necessary and sufficient for our coordinating the predicaments and for producing definitions and for performing the other tasks of the logicians, for the sake of which that division was devised. Then indeed, it can be added that it need not be admitted that not all those branches are specific and ultimate under the concept of "universal" and "predicable." Because in order to have the proper relation of the universal and its essential difference, nothing implies that the inferiors differ among themselves more or less, as long as the relation of the superior to them is of the same mode and nature; however, this happens thus in the case of the alternate and subalternate differences. And the same reasoning holds for "property" and "accident," but not indeed for "genus" and "species" compared to one another, as can stand sufficiently from the reasoning adduced to explain the sufficiency of the division; to explain and discuss this more copiously is not our task.

11. From a second viewpoint, the aforementioned division might seem to be insufficient, since there seem to be other universals which are in no way included in these divisions; these are of two kinds: some are transcendentals which are higher than genera and species, which since they have one objective concept (as has been said above) and are in many things and can be predicated of these, seem to lack nothing for being called universals. Whence, Aristotle IV *Metaphysics* text 10, says "being" and "one" are maximally universals.

12. *Why are the transcendentals not universals?* But it can be answered that transcendentals of this kind are not properly and simply universals, although they are sometimes called thus broadly and in a

[95]

way[37] according to that notion by which everything which is in some way one and is common to many can be called universal. Yet, seeing that they are analogous, they either do not have simple unity or do not refer to the many things equally; hence, they are in that respect excluded from the proper notion and division of the universal which was meant to be divided up through that partition. Whence Aristotle in I *Ethics,* ch. 6, expressly requires for the analysis[38] of the universal that it be univocal, and in 4 *Metaphysics,* ch. 2 he denies that "being" and "one" are universals in this sense. But if you insist that it is not absurd that there be found some objective common concepts, essential to several predicaments and univocal and consequently universal, and yet not generic, since there is no genus which is common to several predicaments (many people think the concept "accident" or the concept "successive being" and the like to be of this sort; these are consequently said not to be genera but in the manner of transcendentals); it is briefly answered that either none of the predicates of this kind are universal (as many want) or certainly if they are such, they are reduced to a genus since they belong with it under the concept "universal" both in the manner of essential predication "*in quid* incompletely" and in not predicating the whole essence of the thing; yet they differ from a proper genus, because they do not have proper differences by which they are contracted; and hence, they do not serve for definitions or for coordinating the predicaments; there will occur below a more appropriate place for speaking of this when we discuss the division of "accident" into the nine predicaments.[39]

13. *Whether a vague individual is a universal.* Otherwise from the other extreme there seem to be some common predicates, as it were lower than in the lowest species, and midway between them and singular determinate individuals, of the type which Cajetan in his chapter on *Species,* thinks is a "vague individual"; and more probably an example can be cited from the common notion of "person," of "supposit" or from the notion of "individual" itself. In reference to this difficulty some people deny that these predicates are univocal. But this is incredible, for it is a fact that "person" is said univocally of any man you choose, and "to be a first substance" is said univocally of any

---

[37] Latin: *secundum quid.*
[38] Literally: "for the notion of the universal." Aristotle is to be imagined here as collecting the concepts which stand as elements in the more complex notion of "universal," the performance of this task is analysis and the last of elemental concepts which are each necessary and together sufficient conditions for "being universal" is called the *analysis.* A similar process is envisioned by Suarez when he discusses the necessity and sufficiency of actual "communication to inferiors" for universality.
[39] This matter is not treated in this work but is discussed in *Disputation XXXIX, De Divisione Accidentis in Novem Summa Genera, op. cit.* (note 1), Vol. 26, p. 504.

first substance; for what aspect of analogy or equivocality can be excogitated in these predicates? Others say they are contained under the universal "species," for the notion of "person" is compared as a specific notion to this and that person, and the notion of "individual" to this or that individual, as it is such. But granted perhaps that this can be defended by formally comparing, for example, the notion of "person" to this person as such, still it does not seem true if the comparison be made to this man as such, because as such it is not a quidditative predicate of him. This can be taken from Aquinas, *Ia*, q. 30, a.4, ad 3. And this is sufficient to constitute a distinct universal with regard to the relation as it is now considered by us. Just as "visible" also is a species with respect to this or that visible thing as such; and nonetheless with respect to this or that man as such it constitutes a new predicable since under that aspect it is not predicated essentially.

14. Therefore it seems it must be said that "individual," as such, does not, with respect to several individuals, constitute a new universal, since from a formal point of view it expresses nothing other than the transcendental unity of each entity as far as it exists in reality; and it is thus excluded, as are the other transcendental predicates. Especially because, if it is understood with regard to whatever positive thing it expresses, it adds nothing beyond "being"; if it is understood with regard to what it formally adds, that is merely a certain negation. Whence among individuals of the same species, for example, two men, when one is exclusively considering their individual essences, there is, beyond the specific agreement, no other in the notion of "individual," except insofar as they agree in the notion of "undivided being"—which is merely transcendental agreement. However, I think that the notion of "person" or "supposit" can be reduced to the predicament of "property," insofar as that mode in which it is constituted, namely, personality or subsistence, is not essential but is by reason of itself alone an accompaniment of the essence, just as to inhere actually can be called a certain proper accident. Nor does this [opinion] take note of the fact that that mode of personality or subsistence is not in its own entity a proper accident but a substantial mode, since this does not vary the mode of universality or predication; just as "to be big-headed," "to be actually two-footed," is called an accident of the fifth predicable, because the mode of predication is accidental and contingent, although the *thing* thus understood is not an accident but a substance; but this is enough on these points.

15. Finally we can add another way of explaining that division of the absolute universal (or the universal inasfar as it arises through the abstractive consideration of the intellect) in which, although the aforesaid members cannot be entirely distinguished with reference to vari-

[97]

ous relations to their inferiors, as the discussion above showed, they can still be distinguished in some way in relation to metaphysical composition. Thus, genus is called that which is disposed to constitute a species in the manner of a potency; difference, that which contracts and divides the genus and constitutes the species in the manner of a form or act; a species will be what is composed of these; a property, what happens to the species by reason of itself; an accident, what contingently "in-exists" in the individual or in the species by reason of the individuals. And yet the universal is not divided in this manner with regard to different notions of universality, but rather with regard to the different *relationships* of universals among themselves. Yet, just as the universal of species might be, as it were, pre-eminent, total and absolute; so the others might express some relationship, quasi-partial or formal, to the species, as has been explained. Whence it is also probable that "universal" under this aspect is not used equally in its primary sense *[aeque primo]* or univocally of these universals, but primarily of those which are essential, next of the others which are outside the essence and, among the former, the universal of species is the pre-eminent; because of this, Plato, as Aristotle sometimes interprets him, posited ideas only of the species. One need not suppose an analogy among "species," "genus" and "difference" with regard to the notion of "universal," since all express agreement and essential unity, and have the same mode of identity with respect to these things from which they are abstracted—something which happens otherwise with "property" and "accident." And this consideration of universals with regard to their proper notions and with respect to that which is distinguished or compared among them, applies especially to knowing and defining the essences of things; therefore it is particularly necessary to the work of metaphysics. Given that "property" and "accident" are indeed outside the essences of things, nothing arises for consideration about them, insofar as they are universals, beyond the intentions and relations of reason which are explained by the logicians in relation to predication, and besides what we shall say below in its place about the proper and real accidental essence, its distinction from substance, and the various relations which it has to substance, among which one can be the "intrinsic connection"[40] on account of which it happens that it is named "property"; of the other three universals, "genus", "species," and "difference," it must further be told how they are distinguished in things and what principle and basis they have in things.

[40] Latin: "dimanatio"; literally, "flowing out of, or from."

SECTION IX

How Unity of Genus and Unity of Difference Are Really Distinguished from One Another, As Well As from the Specific Unity

1. That genus and difference are distinguished in reality, seems to be urged by these arguments: first, the species is composed of genus and difference (which composition is called metaphysical); nor should it be considered entirely fabricated by reason but also in some way found in things themselves; whence the more reliable theologians say it is not to be found in God because it is incompatible with His supreme simplicity; this is a sign, therefore, that genus and difference are in some way distinct in reality itself and not purely by reason in our conceptions, since otherwise they would not bring about composition in a real thing; for a mere distinction of reason, even based on a virtual distinction or upon the eminence of the thing, is not enough for a true composition in a real thing; therefore in the thing there is some distinction between genus and difference. And this is confirmed, for Aristotle in 7 *Metaphysics*, ch. 10, text 33 employed this reason, when he said that a definition must be constructed from parts, namely genus and difference: "The parts of the definition are related to the parts of the thing in just the same way that the definition is related to the whole thing"; there is therefore some true distinction between them, just as between the parts of the thing.

2. The same thing is proved secondly, since things which have essences or parts which are in some way diverse are in some way distinct in reality itself; but genus and difference are thus related: therefore . . . The minor is proved from these things which are commonly attributed to genus and difference. For Aristotle in 3 *Metaphysics*, text 10, says in the first place that the difference is beyond the notion of the genus; therefore the difference is not of the essence of the genus, nor vice versa. Whence, in 6 *Topics*, ch. 3, Aristotle says that genus does not share in the difference nor the difference in the genus; and in 7 *Metaphysics*, ch. 12, text 42, he says that differences are not posited in the notion of the genus, but that the genus is compared to the differences, as a potency to an essential act, and hence there is made of these a thing which is "one" *per se*. It is obvious from reason, for the differences dividing the genus are mutually opposed; therefore they cannot both be of the essence of the genus; therefore neither one nor the other can be of the essence of the genus. The inference is clear, as much because there is no greater reason for one or the other [to be essential to the genus], as, because if one were of the essence, it would

[99]

be inseparable whence the other could never belong to it, since opposites cannot at once inhere in the same thing; therefore the genus has an essence of itself distinct from the differences or not including them. On the other hand, that the difference expresses the essence, not including the genus, is clear, for one reason, because the genus would otherwise be transcendent; also for another reason, because the difference would otherwise include the whole of that which the species includes, whence a certain pointlessness would be achieved when the difference is joined to the genus.

3. A third argument can be that whatever things are separated in reality, must also be in some way distinct in reality; but the higher and lower levels are separated in reality, for one finds the notion of "animal" in some places where "rational" is not found; and so for the others. A like argument is: that in reality two species are alike in generic notion but not in specific; whence it is seen to be necessary that these natures be distinct in reality itself. Again, because the difference contracts the genus and actualizes it; therefore they are not entirely the same thing, because the same thing does not contract itself. I argue forthly, that these locutions are precisely and abstractly false: "Animality is rationality" and the like, and not even on account of a formal distinction, for if the predicate and the subject were entirely the same, the proposition would be affirming the truth; but by these terms the generic and differential levels are precisely signified; therefore these levels are distinguished *ex natura rei*.

4. And it is further concluded here, that the genus and difference taken one by one are distinguished from the whole species *ex natura rei*, since they are compared to it as parts are compared to a whole really and truly composed of them; however, the whole is distinguished "ex natura rei" from the single components, although it is not distinguished from them all taken simultaneously and as united; for it is at least distinguished as including something which the other does not include. Whence for this reason it is also commonly said that genus and difference, taken precisely under the aspect of parts, cannot be predicated truly of the species; for a part is not predicated of the whole. And it is confirmed in the first place, for if "man" and "animal" are in no way distinguished in reality, nor "horse" and "animal" also; then "man" and "horse" could not be distinguished; for whatever things are the same as a third thing are the same among themselves; and whatever is of the essence of one thing will be of the essence of the other and conversely; for if "man" and "animal" are the same in reality, whatever is of the essence of "man" will be of the essence of "animal," and it will be the same with "horse"; therefore it will be the same when we compare "man" and "horse" together. Or, it must certainly be confessed

that something of the essence of "animal" is in "man" but is not in "horse" or conversely; from which it follows that "animal" is not applied univocally or with the same meaning to "man" and "horse," but is used equivocally, or with respect to a paradigm according to a certain analogy of proportionality. Finally it is confirmed by that reason often put forward: that different things cannot in the same respect be entirely similar and different; but two species are simply and essentially different, and yet they are alike in genus; this cannot happen therefore unless "genus" and "species" are in some way distinct in reality.

Various Opinions Are Mentioned

5. In this matter, there can be various ways of talking. The first is, that those levels are not distinguished at all *ex natura rei* but entirely *really*, at least through the inclusion of something really distinct which is in the one and not in the other. Jandun, 2 *Metaphysics*, q.9, indicates this opinion and all those who think those levels, the generic and specific, are taken from really distinct forms ought to hold the same opinion, for it follows thence that "body" means only the composite of matter and corporeal form, "living" means only the composite of body and vegetative soul, that "animal" adds a really distinct sensitive soul, and "man," the rational soul. Concerning the differences, however, ("rational" and the like) this opinion would perhaps say that only the last form is spoken of as informing; whence it also happens to bespeak something really distinct from the genus. And hence Durandus perhaps thought (in II, d.3, q.1) that in simple things like angels and accidents, or the forms themselves, it is impossible to find proper differences and consequently it is not possible to find composition of genus and difference.

6. The second opinion is that these predicates are distinguished from one another *ex natura rei* and also from the composite itself, at least by a formal or modal distinction, as they call it. So Scotus holds in II, d.3, q.1, and VII *Metaphysics*, q.16 and Anthony Andreas, in same book in quest. 7; for although Scotus sometimes posits a real distinction between the common and proper physical forms, as between the form of corporeity and the soul, for example, and then had to say that between the *levels* taken by these forms there was a greater distinction than the formal distinction (in accordance with the preceding opinion), yet Scotus did not think that this real formal distinction was necessary in order to distinguish those levels, for he admits that simply physically, in the same thing, there are both true genus and difference, and the composition of these; and then, generally speaking, he says that a formal distinction *ex natura rei* is sufficient and that it is the necessary medium. It is not sufficiently established whether this formal distinc-

[101]

tion according to Scotus is actual in the thing, or merely virtual or fundamental and thus coincides with the other which is called a "distinction of the reasoning reason," for he speaks varyingly, as we shall point out in the following disputation;[41] for now the opinion is to be treated by us in that sense in which it postulates an actual distinction in reality, and in that sense it seems Ferrara concurs I *Cont. Gent.*, ch. 24 and ch. 42; and Fonseca, 2 *Metaphysics*, chap. 2, text 11, where he culls it from the text of Aristotle who denies that a recession to infinity can be given in essential predicates, because if they were distinguished by thought only, then there would be no problem about finding a process to infinity in them. Fonseca repeats the same point in Book IV, ch. 2, q.4, sect. 3; and Book V, ch. 7, q.3, sect. 3, ad secundum.

7. The third opinion can be the extreme contrary: that these things are distinguished neither in reality nor even in the mind but are entirely the same, although they are signified by different terms. This opinion can be attributed to the nominalists, insofar as they entirely deny that these universals are found in things; it is however scarcely credible that such an opinion has ever come into the mind of any philosopher, as the arguments made in the beginning conclude at a minimum.

8. Therefore the true opinion is that all these things are distinguished by reason, with a certain basis taken from the things themselves, yet that there is not any true and actual or real distinction or distinction *ex natura rei* among all levels of this kind, so far as they exist conjoined on the part of the thing. This is the opinion of St. Thomas, as is established by *Ia*, q.50, a.4, ad 1; q.76, a.3, ad 4, and *De Ente et Essentia* ch. 4 and following; and 7 *Metaphysics*, Lect. 4 and often elsewhere; the Thomists commonly hold the same opinion, Herveus Natalis, *Quodlibet*, 1, q.9; Capreolus, 1, dist. 8, q.2, art. 3; Cajetan, Soncinas and Soto in places cited in the previous section;[42] Greg.[43] in 1, dist. 38; Gab.[44] and other nominalists. And since the affirmative part of the distinction of reason has been evidently proved with the arguments produced and does not involve difficulty, nothing needs to be added; however, the basis of such a distinction will be clarified in the resolutions of the arguments and further in the following section.

The True Opinion Is Explained

9. To prove the other negative part, it must be noticed since we are

[41] *Disputation VII: On the Various Kinds of Distinctions;* complete citation in note 2, above.
[42] It is presumed, since there are no citations of Cajetan, Soncinas and Soto in the preceding section (VIII) or in the one (VII) before that, that

Suarez has in mind the citations in Section VI, Number 2, He might also have in mind the citations given in Section II, Number 8.
[43] Gregory in Rimini.
[44] Gabriel Biel.

concerned with the distinction of these levels of "genus," "difference," and "species," that they can be correlated or compared in four ways: first, as they are found in reality in diverse things or species, as if "animal" which is in a man were compared with the species of a lion or a horse or if "animal" as it is in a lion were compared to the difference "rational," for example, or to another similar difference; this comparison is both outside the matter at hand and irrelevant, for in this sense it stands established that the generic nature existing in a thing can be really distinguished from some difference or its species; the formal unity of the genus itself is multiplied (regarded as a thing) in the different species (just as we have said above that the specific formal unity, as it exists in reality, is multiplied in number in individuals). The answer to whether the genus, insofar as it is in one species in reality, is distinguished from another species or its difference not only really but also essentially and quidditatively, perhaps depends upon the manner of speaking, and depends upon the proof of this opinion; and it is explained in the solutions of the arguments.

10. Secondly, these things can be compared by themselves by our abstracting from existence both in reality and in the intellect, in the way in which we cited several authors as saying that a nature by itself, that is, taken stripped and alone, is universal, as it antecedes every work of intellect; for these people seem to think that quidditative predicates are distinguished in the same sense among themselves *ex natura rei*. For if "animal," for example, has of itself and prior to intellect a positive disposition to various differences and a unity of precision of itself common to many species, it follows necessarily that it has of its own nature some distinction from all the differences by which it is divided and from the species to which it can be contracted. However, if we postulate what we have said about the notion of "universal," then this comparison is irrelevant; for we have shown that there is no state in which a common nature, whatever that be, can have any unity of isolation apart from the intellect, if as it exists in the things themselves, it does not have such unity. For a nature outside the understanding can have only a double state, namely, a state of actual existence and a state of possibility; nor can one excogitate or imagine another middle state; however, a nature as possible is not differently distinguished or isolated from the possible differences or species than is an existing nature from existing species and differences; nor is any possible nature distinct from its individual inferiors or species, if it cannot be distinct in an existing thing; the existing and possible natures are not one thing and another thing, but are the same thing considered in different states; therefore this comparison can be nothing which has a basis in reality.

11. Genus and difference can be compared, thirdly, as much together as with the species which they comprise, so far as they are in an intellect conceiving their singulars precisely and abstractly; and in this way it stands that they are distinguished by reason, as we have said; whether they are distinguished more than by reason (something which is especially to be noted in my attack on the arguments made at the outset) cannot be sufficiently gathered from this comparison alone, unless another sign of a greater distinction be found in the things themselves. It is proved since it is the power of the intellect that it isolate and abstract those things which are not actually distinct or isolated in reality; therefore, from the fact that some things, as objects of the mind are distinguished by reason, it is not possible to conclude to any distinction among them in reality; since to be thus distinguished by reason is nothing other than to be the object of distinct conceptions of the intellect and since something which stands as a whole without distinction in reality may be conceived in a different manner or under a different aspect. And this can be confirmed from what we have said above about the objective concept of "being," about how it is isolated by the intellect and is really distinct from all lower entities; for the reasons given there apply here in the same way, and we shall touch on them briefly below.

12. And then things can also be compared in a fourth way: insofar as they exist in reality in one and the same species and in one and the same individual of such a species; and the comparison is really intended in this sense in the present question; and in this sense we say that, for example, in Peter the sensitive being is not distinguished *ex natura rei* from the rational, nor the level of animal from the level of man, and so on for the rest.

13. *A second important point.* Whence it must be secondly considered that in reality and in the same individual the generic level can be understood to be distinguished from the specific level in two ways: in one way, as a universal from a particular; in the other way, as an individual from another individual at least formally distinct *ex natura rei*. The former manner of distinction would have a place, if it were true that universals existing on the part of the thing are actually and *ex natura rei* distinguished from the individuals in which they exist, and Scotus seems to have proceeded in this manner and to have consequently spoken in this way, since "animal," for example, does not descend to individuals except by means of the species; and hence, if we at once admit that the specific nature as such is *ex natura rei* distinct from the difference by which it is contracted to individuals, then for a like reason it should be called sufficient that the generic nature is in the same way distinct from the differential level before the nature

is contracted to individuals. This manner of distinction does not have a place, if we assume what we have said against Scotus about the nature of universality: that it can in no way be actual in reality, nor can it be in the existing nature in individuals, but that it is as such only abstracted through the intellect. For if the nature in the thing does not have universality, then neither does it have the universality of the genus, the difference, or the species; therefore they cannot be distinguished in reality as one universal from another or as a universal from its inferior. And it is confirmed because the reasons, by which it was shown above that the universal in reality is not distinct from the singular, equally well prove this of any universal whatever, whether generic or specific, with respect to that singular in which it exists; therefore, in reality there can be no distinction between one lower level and a higher, if both be taken universally, since on the part of the thing they are not distinguished from the singulars.

14. Therefore only one other manner of distinction remains to be examined, and if it be excluded, it will have been satisfactorily shown that there is no distinction between these levels *ex natura rei*. And on this point there is some danger and a greater difficulty in the present question than in that one treated above concerning the distinction of the universal from the individual difference; for if we separate the individual difference, there does not remain a singular and individual thing, and hence there cannot remain an existing thing which is in reality distinguished from such a difference; but in the present case, if we cut off the specific difference, the generic level can be understood, not only in the universal, but in the individual also, as really existing; for Peter, for example, is not only *this* man, but also *this* animal, and *this* rational thing; and hence, if the specific difference be separated by the understanding, it is still possible to understand the generic level as existing in the individual and singular, and accordingly the question still has a place: "How are 'this animal' and 'this man' or 'this rational thing' distinguished in the individual?" It must be proved that they are not distinguished in reality otherwise than from this universality.

15. Therefore it can be first proved from individuation: that in one individual there is entirely one and the same and most simple individual difference proximately and immediately contracting the last species and with it and through it determining, consequently, all higher levels; therefore these levels cannot be distinguished among themselves more than each is distinguished from its individual difference; but none of them is distinguished *ex natura rei* from its individual difference, as has been proved; therefore neither are they distinguished *ex natura rei* in the same individual. The first antecedent is common to

[105]

the logicians and metaphysicians, as Fonseca indicates and explains extensively in Book V ch. 28, q.14, sect. 3, where he shows that a genus is not related to individuals except through the mediation of a species. And the reason is, first, that the generic notion, taken precisely, is indifferent, and as it were, in essential potency to being determined through a specific difference, and hence until it is understood as determined in this way, it is not proximately capable of individuation. Secondly, there is not a less essential relation between generic difference, specific difference, and individual difference, than among the higher essential differences, more and less universal even up to the specific; but "body," for example, is not apt to be contracted through the difference of "animal," except through the medium of the difference "living"; nor "vegitative" through the difference "rational" except through the medium of "sentient"; therefore, neither is "animal" determinable through the individual difference of "this animal," for example, of Peter, except through a mediating difference, "man" or "rational;" therefore there is one entirely indivisible individual difference, which by contracting "man" to "this man," likewise contracts "animal" to "this animal," and so on for the other higher predicates.

Whence, I argue thirdly, that one individual and indivisible difference of this kind is sufficient to determine in the singular the whole and integral essence of a thing, as it includes all predicates specific, generic or higher which can be abstracted or excogitated in it; therefore it would be superfluous to imagine several metaphysical differences of this kind in the same individual. And this is confirmed by an example; for this animal, for instance, which is Peter, is entirely, intrinsically and, as it were, essentially determined to be Peter; and hence it is entirely absurd to think of this individual animal outside of this individual man; and the same is the case with the other higher predicates; therefore it is a sign that "animal" is not determined immediately and by itself to "this animal," but only insofar as it is determined to be "this man;" therefore the same individual difference is determined to the being of this man and of this animal.

16. It is yet confirmed; for an individual thing as such, is understood to be proximately capable of existence; for the universal as such, that is, in its universality, cannot exist; and hence the more universal some predicate is thought to be, the more it, as such, is conceived to be removed from existence; as, for example, "substance in common" is not understood as apt for existing except it be determined to a material or immaterial substance; and the rationale is the same for the whole series of general predicates, even down to the last species, which is proximately capable of existence when contracted to its individual; therefore, just as no individual can exist unless it be in some lowest

[106]

species, as is most certain (especially ignoring the false opinion about the real distinction of several substantial forms essentially subordinated in the same composite), so no generic notion is understood to be determined to a proper individual except it be contracted and determined to some species. This is seen to be quite evident especially in simple things, both whole and partial; for who imagines or mentally conceives Michael, for example, to be this substance, this spirit, and this Angel through another thing? Or the rational soul of Peter to be this soul and this rational soul through another thing? And so on for the others. Indeed, in such cases, one cannot satisfactorily conceive, through a mental abstraction, "this individual" as existing under the generic notion and not under some specific notion as, for instance, "this existing substance," while not thinking of "this body" or "this spirit." Therefore let it be established that all the essential attributes in one and the same individual are individuated by a unique singular difference in the final specific notion. From this it is clearly concluded (something we were in the first inference deducing) that the essential attributes in the same individual cannot be more distinguished among themselves than they are from the individual difference; since that is one and indivisible; therefore the things which are individuated through it cannot be distinguished as two individuals distinct *ex natura rei* since in distinct individuals there must also be found distinct individual differences in the very way in which they are different; again, whatever things are entirely the same *ex nature rei*, with the same individual and indivisible difference, cannot be individually distinguished one from another; so they are in no way distinguished *ex natura rei* since as was proved, a distinction *ex natura rei* cannot intervene, except between individual and singular things as such.

SECOND PROOF

17. The assertion put forth is proved secondly, since in one individual, for example, in Peter, to be "this animal" and to be "this man" result from the same physical principle, namely, from *this soul*, as is self-evident, and will be expatiated in the next section; but in *this soul*, for example, of Peter, the rational or sensitive and vegitative being (whether formally or eminently) are not *ex natura rei* distinct levels; therefore the levels of "man" and "animal" are not in any way distinct in Peter; consequently, it is clear that we rightly concluded that "this animal" is not really distinguished from "this man", for *this soul* which gives the animal-being is not really distinct from that which gives the being-of-this-man. So in this way it is concluded that it is not to be distinguished *ex natura rei*. You may say that this argument proceeds from what is equally unknown; for whoever posits this distinction in the composite also posits it in the form, and in whatever other thing,

[107]

even if it be physically simple. It is replied that, granted that one consequently must talk this way according to this opinion, yet the argument and the difficulties are justly reduced to the roots of these levels and to simple physical entities, since in their case it can appear the more clearly how superfluously and causelessly this distinction is imagined: there is no sufficient indication of it [this distinction] in the basis and root of such levels. This is obvious, for the rational soul, for example, is one simple form in reality; if this is considered as the efficient principle of all operations which are in man, it is thought to be the one eminent and, as it were, universal principle of them; nor must various entities or real modes distinct *ex natura rei* be imagined in the soul through which it might be the chief and root principle of such operations; otherwise various levels or modes of being distinct *ex natura rei* would also have to be imagined in the form, or in the light of the sun insofar as it is the universal principle of several actions. And it would have to be similarly philosophized in the case of every general principle of several actions or effects: something which is foreign to every reason and right conception since "what are distinct in inferiors are united in a higher principle." Therefore the rational soul, through its being which is entirely the same and entirely simple in reality, is the root principle of all human operations without there being any actual distinction in it, so that it has the nature of such a simple principle, although it can be multiply conceived by us through inadequate concepts and can be thus distinguished by reason in relation to various operations. Therefore the same soul in the same manner, in the genus of formal cause, confers upon man all the levels of "living," "animal," and "man," with regard to entirely the same reality and without any actual distinction *ex natura rei* being found in it. The inference is clear, as much because the notion of the soul is the same whether one or the other kind of cause be considered; as, also because the soul is the basic principle of operations on account of the very same respect in which it is the principle which formally constitutes the operating thing. Moreover, these levels are not distinguished by us in the soul otherwise than in relation to its operations. Whence, if there is not necessarily a distinction in relation to those operations, found naturally in their principle, it will not be necessary in the notion of the informing principle.

18. But if there is not necessarily a distinction *ex natura rei* in these levels which are considered in relation to their diverse operations, much less will there necessarily be one in the other higher or lower genera or differences, as are, for instance, the notion of "body" or "substance"; or, if we talk of forms, the notion of "substantial form" or "form of the body." For by the very fact that something is a form

of matter, actualizing its substantial potency, it is a substantial form and it is also the form of the body; this latter is inseparable and indistinguishable *ex natura rei* from whatever form is actuating the matter and composing one composite substance with it. Similarly the lower genera (as is the notion of "brute" under "animal" and others of this kind) can be less distinguished than the aforementioned levels in man; for if a distinction *ex natura rei* is not found in the soul of man considered as principle of varying operations, then it will be much less to be found in the soul of a brute, for example, in relation to its sensitive operations produced in such a way, at this level, and in this order.

THIRD PROOF

19. The third is the best *a priori* reason: this abstraction of genera and species, as it happens through the intellect, has a sufficient base, both in itself and in real things, without any actual distinction which precedes in the real things themselves; therefore such a distinction ought not to be claimed. The inference is proved because the whole reason for introducing this distinction has always been taken from our manner of conceiving and consequently from our manner of speaking as founded upon our manner of conceiving; therefore if a distinction in it is not necessary on account of this cause, then, neither ought it to be believed since real distinctions or distinctions *ex natura rei* are not to be multiplied without foundation. First, however, the antecedent is proved and briefly explained although it was already proved when we were treating the concept of "being" and when we were treating the identity between common nature and individuals. Agreement on the part of the things and an actual similarity more or less perfect along with some dissimilarity and disagreement, is sufficient for the intellect to extract and form those concepts; on the part of the intellect it is sufficient that it can conceive that in which the things agree, in the manner of one thing, by conceiving it in isolation; but this can happen without there being in the thing any actual distinction of these levels. Therefore . . . The minor is proved with the examples cited above; for two men agree together in the notion of "man" and are distinguished as they are individuals, without distinction in reality between the common notion and the individual difference. Again, God and creatures agree under the aspect of a "real being" and differ in the notion of "such a being," without there being a distinction between common and proper notion, either on the part of God (as is certain) or on the part of the creature since no level[45] if it be positive and real, can be isolated in a creature which does not have that agreement with God in the notion of "being." Therefore, these examples declare that exactly the

[45] Latin: *"gradum";* literally, "grade," as in expressions of the form, "the grades of being or perfection."

same thing can be the principle and basis of agreement and difference with another thing because of a greater or less likeness with it, without any actual distinction which precedes in these things.

20. This holds true not only in an analogous agreement, as some interpret it, but also in a univocal one, as the example of specific agreement and individual difference sufficiently shows, and other examples of the more universal or generic agreements can be brought forward; for common sense, for example, works with sight in the perception of colors and thence the common concept can be easily abstracted; it works with hearing in the perception of sound and thence another concept can be abstracted; however, no one will say that the power of perceiving sound and color are distinguished *ex natura rei* in common sense itself. It is the same with the light of the sun, insofar at it works with heat in effecting warmth, and with dryness in drying out. Again the medium qualities between extreme contraries, as red or green color, between whiteness and blackness, and liberality between avarice and prodigality, have a certain agreement and an unfittingness with the extremes; for if liberality be compared to avarice, it differs from it and agrees with prodigality in the force and propensity to spread itself out and communicate itself; compared to prodigality, it differs from it in moderation and agrees with avarice in retaining; however it would be foolish to imagine that there are various levels or real modes distinct *ex natura rei* in liberality, because of these comparisons and conceptions of our intellect which (if the matter is attentatively considered) can be multiplied almost to infinity and differences can scarcely be thought of simple enough so that the intellect cannot further divide them by finding in them some agreement and difference with other things, as in "man," considered as "rational," it finds an agreement with "Angel" in understanding and a difference in the *manner* of understanding; and thus with the others. It is established well enough from these considerations that this kind of concept of the intellect is not a sufficient sign of an actual distinction of real things.

Dismissal of the Arguments

21. *Composition of genus and difference, composition of reason.* It it replied to the first argument proposed at the beginning, that the composition of genus and difference is not real composition but merely of reason; as the argument well proves, true composition and composition in reality cannot be understood without a distinction *ex natura rei;* for composition is nothing other than the union of distinct things; therefore, where there is no distinction in reality, there can be no composition; therefore this is composition of reason. However, this composition is said not to be entirely constructed by reason, not because it actually precedes in reality, but because a basis exists in

reality, whereby the intellect can conceive one notion as potential and isolated from the other, and another as actual and determining the other; and thus the composition is properly merely in the concepts, and is in reality only through extrinsic denomination from concepts of the mind and is, in this sense, said to be composition of reason. Concerning this, composition of this kind is not repugnant to God because of simplicity alone, as I shall say below, but also by reason of the divine illimitation and eminence. For in the first place, on account of this, He cannot have a univocal agreement with creatures; and consequently cannot have generic agreement. Next, no common notion can be so abstracted and isolated in God that it is not included in any proper and particular notion, because of the supreme illimitation and simplicity, which is also incompatible with composition of genus and difference.

22. *The definition and its parts insofar as the parts of the thing are commensurated with them.* It is replied to the confirmation that the parts of the definition are not properly said to refer to parts of the thing, but to have a certain proportion to the parts of the thing, as D. Thomas explains in 7 *Metaphysics,* since genus and difference are related as matter and form, which are the parts of the thing from which the genus and the difference are said for this reason to be taken, as we shall explain more fully in the following section. Next it is said that definition is the work of the intellect and necessarily requires some true and proper composition of distinct concepts, just as a definition put forth by the voice must consist of distinct partial expressions; for it distinctly explains the nature of a thing—something which cannot be done by us in one expression or with one simple concept; and for this reason it is said to be constituted of parts; yet it is not necessary for the singular parts of the definition to explain the single really distinct parts of the defined, but only that together it can express the nature or entity of the defined; nevertheless, the one expresses it confusedly and under the aspect of what is common and potential, the other under the aspect of the more determinate and proper; and notions, diverse in this way, can be called parts of the defined, not *secundum rem* but with regard to reason only; for the defined as *defined* implies the denomination of reason.

23. It is answered to the second objection that genus and difference express essences or essential notions which are diverse with respect to reason but not in reality; and in this sense, a genus is said to be outside the notion of the difference, and the difference is also said to be outside the notion of the genus; for the notion of each is so conceived mentally and isolated in such a way that with regard to that abstraction and isolation neither is formally included in the other; it is not

necessary for this that they be distinct in reality in one and the same thing; but from the point of view of the genus, it is enough that its notion, as it responds to such a conception, is not constituted intrinsically through its divisive difference, and consequently that it can be found in reality without such a difference. On the side of the difference, however, in order for the genus to be said to be outside its notion, it is sufficient that in its precise objective concept there should be included no objective concept of the genus but that the difference be conceived as the act of a genus entirely distinct by reason. And this is enough for genus and species to be said to be compared as potency and essential act, not with respect to the real thing but only with respect to reason; for of whatever kind be the composition, of such a kind ought the acts and potency to be; however, this [in a definition] is composition of reason, as we have said; therefore it [the definition] is said in the same sense to be composed into one thing *per se* of genus and difference, with regard to reason, and not with regard to the thing; and hence such a composite is especially one *per se*, because the components are one in reality, and are compared and subordinated through reason. And in this sense, St. Thomas in 7 *Metaphysics*, Lecture 12 says that the difference is not added to the genus as an essence different from it, but as contained in it implicitly, just as what is determined is contained in what is undetermined; and from this cause, one thing *per se* is composed from these elements.

24. It is answered to the reasoning, that we can speak of genus and difference in two senses. First, as they exist from the point of view of the thing; secondly as they are isolated through the understanding. In the prior sense, since genus and difference are not in reality distinguished in each species, the genus and difference have the same essence as the species, although it is diversely signified through the concepts or words signifying the genus and difference, as St. Thomas, cited above, has said. And "genus" in this sense, as it is in reality, actually includes opposed differences, as it is in different species; in this sense, equivocations are said to lie in the genus. And Aristotle also speaks thus, 10 *Metaphysics* ch. 11, text 24, saying that the genus as it is existing in one species is different from itself as it exists in another. Nor is it an obstacle that those differences are opposed, since the genus thus considered does not have a real unity but has its formal unity multiplied in diverse species, and hence can actuate opposed differences in them, or rather, can be identified with them. However, in the second sense, and we speak more properly and in accordance with the usage of "genus" and "difference," we can take them as they stand as subjects for our abstract and isolated concepts; and thus, only what is *per se* necessary to the foundation and constitution of the thing as

[112]

thus conceived can be said to be of the essence of each thing; and in this sense (as has been said) the divisive differences are not of the essence of the genus, nor the genus of the essence of the differences; yet this whole distinction and precision is through the operation of the intellect to which it expresses a relation (or involves one), and the essence is established when it is signified by the names of the genus and difference.

25. The third argument and all the points indicated in it has often been destroyed in what has gone above, for the same arguments are used in discussing the species with relation to individuals and "being" with respect to its inferiors. Therefore I say that genus, as conjoined with its difference is on the part of the thing inseparable from it; and we say that it is not in reality distinguished from such a difference; that the genus as it is in one species, is separable in reality from a difference of another species, is no argument that in one and the same species, the genus and difference are distinguished, since the genus as it is in one species in reality, and in another, is not really one and the same but is the same only by reason and abstraction; therefore only a distinction of reason is included, for which there is some basis in the reality itself, undoubtedly some incomplete and imperfect similarity of different natures, which can obtain in reality without an actual distinction, as has been explained. Therefore that locution, "the difference contracts or actuates the genus," expresses a relationship to our concepts and hence a distinction of reason suffices for its truth and propriety.

26. The fourth argument touches upon a difficulty which is put forth in the following section; the other arguments which were brought out to show that there is a distinction *ex natura rei* between genus and species, and between difference and species, have an easy solution from what has been said. Whence, it is answered to the first that genus and difference are not compared to the species as parts distinct *ex natura rei* but as parts distinct only by reason. And [it is answered] that this is enough so that a genus or a species taken in isolation cannot be predicated of a species, as has been insisted. The solution of the first confirmation is also obvious from what has been said; for granted that in a man, "animal" is the same as "man," and in a horse it is the same as "horse," it does not follow that "man" and "horse" are mutually the same, because they are not really one animal but only have a likeness in the being-of-animal by reason of which they convene in the one concept of "animal"; and this is sufficient for "animal" to be univocal, and to be used with the same concept of both things although in reality "animal" has a different *real* essence in a man than it has in a horse, and conversely. The assumption of the last confirmation is

[113]

denied; for nothing renders it absurd, as has often been shown, that a thing entirely the same and without any distinction which is in it *ex natura rei*, should be the basis of a similarity and difference with respect to another; since they can be assimilated imperfectly and only "after a fashion," and still simply differ.

Section X

Whether the Metaphysical Abstractions of Genera, Species and Difference Can Be Predicated Mutually

1. I call those things "metaphysical abstractions" which are abstracted by metaphysical concepts, like "animality," "rationality," and the like; I call them "metaphysical abstractions" so as to distinguish them from physical abstractions, like "white," "color," etc., about which there is no doubt as to whether true and proper predications can be made, like "White is a color," etc. Concerning the former terms and the propositions which are constructed from them, like "Animality is rationality" and the like, Scotus (in 1, d.2, q.7; and d.5, q.1; and *Praedicabilibus*, q.16, thought them false because the distinction of the extremes is formal and *ex natura rei*. Indeed Soto in question 3, *Universalibus*, a.2, says Scotus differs on this point from all the Realists; whence he holds the contrary opinion from exactly the opposite premise, namely: that a distinction of reason alone is not sufficient for the falsity of a proposition.

2. But not only Scotus, other writers also think these expressions are to be denied, not because of a distinction *ex natura rei* but because of the mode of signifying which, joined to a distinction of reason, suffices to produce a false proposition when one formal notion, conceived in isolation, is predicated of another distinct by reason, likewise conceived in isolation—which happens in these locutions. Abstract terms refer to isolated formal notions, whence, when one is predicated of the other, it is meant that one is the other, not only with respect to the reality, but also with respect to the isolation of the mind and with regard to reason—which is false; and in this sense Niphus (Bk. 3 *Metaphysics*, d.2) and Cajetan (*De Ente et Essentia*, ch. 4) hold this opinion; and St. Thomas means this in the same work, chs. 3 and 4; and it can be confirmed, since these abstractions refer to the nature in the manner of a part; but one part cannot be truly predicated of another nor of the whole; therefore it is commonly said that even the genus itself, for instance, "animal," if it is taken precisely in the manner of a part, cannot be truly predicated of the species and can only be truly predicated

insofar as it at least confusedly refers to the whole which is in the species or because it adequately signifies that which has such a nature: that is, the whole thing itself. Therefore, if those propositions are taken in the abstract, they can all the less be verified.

3. Perhaps you may object: Why, if there can be predications of this kind involving abstractions of accidents, can they not occur involving abstractions of substances? It is answered from Scotus that these abstractions are the ultimate in abstraction, that is, in such abstraction that they cannot be further abstracted or resolved into other more abstract things; the accidents which are signified in the abstract according to common usage, and concerning which we say these predications can be made, are not abstractions of the highest abstraction; for they might be further resolved or abstracted, as if from "white," "whiteness" is abstracted, and from "color," "coloriety"; for then in these abstractions the aforementioned predications also could not be made; for the same cause militates against it. More properly or formally it might be said that the reason is the same for substances and accidents, if the abstraction be of the same degree, namely, either physical or metaphysical; indeed, there is between these a diverse degree. For, by physical abstraction, namely of "white" from a subject, the essence is not abstracted from the very thing itself which it constitutes (if I may speak thus) but a form is abstracted from a subject; and hence, by force of such abstraction only universal predication in the manner of "property" or "accident" is taken away, since as such, such a form can be predicated neither of its subject nor of the composite, because it is compared to the latter as a part, and to the former as something distinct from it, and it is not referred to as existing in it but as standing by itself. Next, as such it does not refer in any way to the thing having the form, nor does it stand for it, but only for the form itself which it refers to. And the like of this will be the case for substances, if we abstract the form from the composite, and signify it abstractly, such as the soul from the animated, etc.; for what is thus abstracted will not be able to be predicated of the concrete; [yet] among abstractions, predications of the higher can be made of the lower; for "soul" is rightly predicated of such and such a soul. Through the other, *metaphysical* abstraction, the essence is abstracted from the entity which it constitutes and it [the essence] is formally conceived and signified, as when "whiteness" is discussed; and hence among these abstractions true predications cannot be made when the notions concerned are distinct at least according to reason.

4. The last among these opinions attains the greatest truth; yet, to explain the matter more fully, we can distinguish here four kinds of predications: for in the first place, the higher and quasi-generic ab-

[115]

straction can be predicated of the lower abstraction, as if of the specific and integral, as when we say: "Humanity is animality," Secondly, the same generic abstraction can be predicated of an abstraction, not of a species, but merely of a difference, which is compared to something, as the formal is to the material, as if we should say: "Rationality is animality." Thirdly, this formal abstraction or differential abstraction can be, on the other hand, predicated of the specific abstraction, as in this statement: "Humanity is rationality." Fourthly, the same abstraction of the difference can be asserted of the generic or material abstraction, as in the predication: "Animality is rationality."

5. Beginning with this last predication: it seems to me, strictly speaking, false because of the reasons given; and because those two extremes, as precisely and abstractly signified, may in no way be compared so that one might be formally included in the other; and consequently one cannot express that whole which the other expresses, either actually or potentially, or explicitly or confusedly. And although animality and rationality are sometimes identical in the same essence, yet this is not meant by *that* manner of speaking, but it rather appears as if the predication were of the formal and quidditative concept of the subject. From this an excellent confirmation arises, because rationality cannot be truly predicated of animality except as a difference dividing it and contracting it, and moreover, existing outside its notion; but it is not predicated as a dividing difference in that locution, because a dividing difference, since it is outside the genus, adds to it and is related like an accident, and hence cannot be predicated of it in the abstract, but only in the concrete. Because of this fact, Avicenna rightly says in tract 5 of his *Metaphysics,* ch. 6, that rationality, as it is signified in the abstract, is not a difference, but the *principle* of a difference. And on account of the same cause, I think the third locution is, strictly speaking, false because in it also "rationality" is not predicated as a difference, since it is not predicated *in quale;* therefore it is predicated as the whole and integral notion of humanity and thus produces a false meaning. Likewise, I think that expressions of the second kind are strictly speaking false, although in the identical sense, they are less indirect than the first, for every essence which is really "rationality" is also "animality"; indeed, the converse is not so.

6. But expressions of the first kind seem to be able to admit some true sense in all rigor and propriety, although they appear equivocal and hence are not to be admitted without distinction. For "humanity," when it expresses the entire essence and nature of man, includes in its concept "animality" and "rationality," because this whole is of the essence of man. Again, "humanity" does not mean "rationality" alone; for its concept includes more, as is self-evident; it expresses not only

the ultimate difference of man, and not only the abstraction of the difference, but expresses the form of the whole thing which physically includes the whole nature composed of matter and form and metaphysically all the levels of such a nature. Therefore, "humanity" is really a certain sensitive nature and has in this fact some agreement and similarity with the nature of "horse" and of "lion", taken in the abstract; for all are the integral principle of "being sentient"; therefore one common concept which is generic to them and can be predicated of them can be abstracted from them all; and in a confused manner and in potency, it may express that whole which is found in the single members; and plainly, this concept seems to signify in that expression, the integral principle or whole of "being sentient," which is undoubtedly truly predicated of all those natures. Therefore if by the term "animality" the same concept is signified in the same way, it will be a true locution. However, this meaning does not seem foreign to the proper use of that term; because, granted that that abstraction is meant as a part with respect to the concrete thing and hence cannot be truly predicated of it (according to the better opinion treated below in the disputation concerning supposition), yet with respect to the very total form itself, (even though it does not formally express the whole of its notion) yet it still seems able to refer confusedly to that whole or to its common concept as including all its determinations in potency; in that sense, that proposition will be therefore true; just as this is also true: "This humanity of Christ is humanity," and pertains to predicating the species of the individual.

7. Nonetheless, there can be an equivocation on that word "animality" because of the formal signification and precision of an abstract term, so that by it may be meant the constuitive notion of "animal," as isolated from all inferiors; and in this sense the expression would be false as the arguments produced earlier entail; and hence, that expression would not be one to be admitted without distinction; and with regard to this, the reason is not the same as for the common physical abstractions of forms or accidents; for since these are by their nature real and physical forms, when they are signified or conceived in the abstract, they are plainly understood to be abstracted from subjects, not to be isolated from all lower differences; however, the substantial nature is merely a metaphysical form and is not properly in a subject, and hence, when it is conceived and referred to in the abstract, it seems to be referred to with complete precision from every contracting characteristic, according to that opinion of Avicenna: "Horseness is merely horseness," although it is not absurd for it to be referred to in the manner of a potential whole with respect to the inferiors, as we have said. But you may ask: if "animality" can be conceived in this

[117]

sense as the genus of humanity and of other natures taken in the abstract, why will "rationality" not have the aspect of a difference, or what will be its difference? The answer is that if someone wishes to define humanity metaphysically, he will understand it easily; for he will not say that humanity is "animality rationality"; for it would be an incongruous expression; nor would that be a definition, because those two parts are in no way conjoined to form one statement. Therefore he will say that humanity is "rational animality." "Rational" is therefore the difference even of that abstraction, since, as I was saying above, the abstraction as such cannot be predicated in the manner of a difference but of a genus or species; for it is always predicated *in quid;* predication *in quale* is produced only through connotative or objective terms which refer to the form *as informing* or being added to another. And hence also among the accidents, although the genus is predicated in the abstract of the species, a difference is never expressed in the manner of an abstraction, but in the manner of a concrete: for we would not say that white is color and disturbance of sight, but a disturbing color, or a disturbing sight. But if you still object that the difference cannot be the same for the genus taken in the abstract and in the concrete, it is answered that "rational" conjoined to "animal" in the concrete, and to "animality" in the abstract, is not attributed to both in the same sense; for in the one it means that there is merely a rational nature, in the other that there is a rational supposit.

SECTION XI

What Is the Principle of the Formal and Universal Unity in Things

1. Although universal unity differs in some way from formal unity, as we have said, yet because it is not unity from the point of view of the thing but rather from the point of view of reason, there is not in reality a different principle for each unity, and hence it is not necessary to raise diverse questions about them; but with the principle of formal unity explained, the principle of universal unity will have been explained, since this is not based in things except through the medium of formal unity. And hence Ferrara rightly says, in 2 *Cont. Gent.,* ch. 95, when he asks what genus and difference are taken from, that inquiry must not be pursued "second intentionally" concerning genus and species, that is, as they have a unity or relation of reason through the mind, but that the inquiry must be made "first intentionally," that is, with respect to the formal unity or agreement which they can have

in reality. Here the discussion is concerned with the physical principle; for just as in the preceding sections, after explaining individual unity, we sought out and explained its principle, that is, the physical basis which it has in reality, so here we are looking for a similar principle, with respect to formal unity, which is either the unity of the genus, of the difference, or of the species composed of both; I now omit formal transcentental unity because it is either analogous and is thus not simply unity or, if it be univocal, can then be reduced to generic unity, as I said above, and has the same relational basis as I shall explain.

2. Thus, the clarified question coincides with the common question: Whence do genus and difference arise? And there is a reason for doubting, since it is common custom to say that genus is taken from the matter and difference from the form; something which nevertheless does not appear true. First, because formal unity of genus and species is also found in angels, and yet neither matter nor form is found in them. Secondly, because, if the genus is taken from the matter, then whatever did not have common matter could not have a common genus; the consequent is clearly false, since it is both the case that material substances agree in some genus with immaterial substances, and that terrestrial bodies agree in some genus with celestial ones, although they do not share in matter. Thirdly, even in substances having similar matter, the genera are not taken from the matter, as is clear for the genus of "living," "animal" and the like; for the living does not receive its life from the matter but from the form; and so on of the others. On the other hand, there is the fact that this is the manner of speech of almost all the ancients, especially St. Thomas, *De Ente et Essentia*, chs. 4, 5 and 6 and 2 *Cont. Gent.*, ch. 95, and *De Spiritualibus Creaturis*, article 1; and Averroes, in 10 *Metaphysics* at the end of Commentary 96 indicates this, because of Aristotle's saying here: "the corruptible and incorruptible differ in genus," as a result of the fact that they also differ in matter. In saying this, he means either that the genus is the matter or that the genus must be taken entirely from the matter.

THE EARLIER OPINION IS REJECTED

3. There can be two ways of talking about this point. The first is that the matter and the form, taken properly and strictly, are proper and necessary principles of the formal generic or specific unity; and that, in this sense, the genus is taken from the physical matter as from a proper principle, while the difference or the species (these two are used for the same thing, since the difference constitutes the species) is taken from the form. And those who deny that immaterial things are composed of genus and difference, but say only things composed of matter and form are, seem to think in this manner. Among these is

[119]

Durandus (in 2, d.3, q.1); and they cite Albert (in *Predicamentis,* the chapter on *Substance);* and in the same place, Giles of Rome (and in his *Quodlibet* 1, q.8); for those moved by this reasoning (as it appears) deny that corporeal substances are univocally substances with the incorporeal things. Averroes *(loco. supra. cit.),* also denied this of the terrestrial and celestial bodies, since he thought the heavens did not consist of matter—concerning which, elsewhere. It is true that it does not follow necessarily from this principle that these authors denied that there were genera and differences in the angels and heavens, since they could have thought them to have among themselves a generic agreement, even if they denied they had it with lower substances. Yet, if they thought thus, they were able to find no probable reason on account of which they might deny common genera to these substances composed of matter and form and to those immaterial substances which admit composition of genus and difference; just as in this respect they are like lower substances, so they can have some union and generic agreement with them; nor will this be incompatible with their simplicity or perfection; therefore they will consequently say more: that, by this fact that they do not have matter and form, neither can they have genus and difference because the latter are based upon the former. However, I do not see what basis could be alleged for the assertion thus explained, except that just as matter is in potency to several forms and composes diverse essences with it, so the genus is related to several differences. But this opinion thus explained is clearly false, as the arguments produced at the beginning and those which we have brought forth, entail; and that basis is especially weak, since that agreement is not through a true likeness of property but merely through some kind of proportion.

RESOLUTION OF THE QUESTION

4. *The genus which is said to be taken from matter, the difference from the form.*—There is therefore a second opinion that matter and form, not with respect to physical propriety, but with regard to a certain proportion and analogy are the principles from which genus and difference are taken. For matter is the first and, as it were, essential or substantial potency of the substantial nature, indifferent of itself to several natures or acts; the form is the first substantial act determining or constituting the nature. Therefore, since the genus is something potential and indifferent and is actualized through the difference and determined to a certain level or species of nature, it is thus said that the genus is taken from the matter and the difference from the form; that is, through a certain proportion to matter and form. And this is the opinion of Aristotle (8 *Metaphysics,* text 6) and St. Thomas, (mentioned, *Opusculum de Ente et Essentia,* and 2 *Cont. Gent.,* ch. 95 and

7 *Metaphysics,* lect. 11 and 12, and in other places to be cited below). And in this sense it is true and obvious. Therefore it must be said, speaking in general, that the principle of formal unity is the whole essence and nature of the thing, yet in a differing way, for the principle of generic unity is the nature itself as further perfectible and determinable or insofar as it has an agreement and similarity with other things in some potential or further determinable level. However, specific unity or the unity of the difference is the nature itself with respect to its ultimate essential perfection. It is proved first by the reasons given, since it is not possible to assign another mode which is common to all substances and accidents and forms. Secondly, since in the material substances themselves neither form nor matter is the sufficient principle of genus and difference; because, as was said above, both genus and difference express in some way the whole nature of the thing and hence can be predicated of the species. Whence, if, *per impossibile,* we were to think of a composite of a rational soul, and another matter of another type from this in which man now consists, then from such a matter and form, the genus and difference in which man essentially consists now would not arise; since "rational" granted that it is chiefly taken from the soul, nevertheless includes such matter essentially. And on the contrary, although this matter be imagined without composition with any form, no proper genus of substance can be taken from it, except perhaps the genus of the matter, with respect to which the matter itself is related as the whole nature by which (as it has agreement with the matter of heaven in some further determinable level) such an incomplete genus can be taken; and consequently, from the same matter, as it has a complement in its essence, is taken the ultimate difference constituting the species of such matter; and in its way, it is the same with the form; therefore in any thing, every unity of this kind is taken from the whole nature compared or conceived in one way or another. However, this must be interpreted with due care, for in the case of complete and integral substances, it is true simply and with every propriety, since they are what have proper and integral natures. Since generic and specific unity is found in its own way in partial substances (as are matter and form) also, it must be understood in these cases according to a proportion with regard to the different aspects of this sort that genus and difference are taken from the whole nature, namely, the whole partial nature; that is, from the total entity of the form or matter; something which is also accomodated in the same way to accidental forms, as can be widely seen in St. Thomas, *Opusc. De Ente et Essentia,* chapter 7.

REPLIES TO THE ARGUMENTS

5. *Genera and differences are truly found in angels.*—To the first

[121]

argument, we therefore grant that there are genera and species in the angels, as St. Thomas often declares (in the mentioned *Opusculum de Ente et Essentia*, chs. 5 and 6 and in *Ia*, q.50, a.2, ad 1, and other places), as we shall treat below when discussing intelligences.[46] There need not be matter and form in them, since, as we have said, they are not always the principles of genus and difference, but the principle is a certain nature, even simple, as long as it is such that it can have a universal agreement with other things in some level abstractable by the intellect as determinable or determining. It is not absurd that this be found in angelic natures since they are finite and limited in perfection. You may say: therefore there is no difference between material and immaterial substances in this; since in both genus and species arise from the whole nature according to the more perfect or more imperfect level, whence they appear as matter and form, as it were, accidentally, since they only come together inasfar as they are parts composing such a nature. The consequent, however, seems opposed to the cited positions of St. Thomas, especially *Ia*, q.5, a.2, ad 1, where he says there is a difference between material and immaterial substances, because in the former the genus is taken from the one thing and the difference from another; in the latter, both are taken from one and the same thing according to diverse aspects. Fonseca replies, as cited above, that if we speak of the proximate principle, there is no difference, because it is the whole nature in every substance, as we have said; if we talk of the root principle, there is some difference on this point; for in immaterial substances, since they are not composed of physical parts, the root principle is the same as what is proximate principle of all formal unity; however, in material substances since they are comprised of physical parts, although the whole nature is the proximate principle, matter is thought to be the root principle of the genus, since it is the root of the whole potentiality, and since the genus through a proportion to it is considered as determinable through differences; the form is thought to be the first root of "difference," since it gives the final perfection and reduces the entire nature to act. In this regard a difference can also be considered between the matter and the form, since matter of itself is not properly the root cause of any level, even of the generic, unless it is actualized through a form upon which every level of the substantial nature primarily and essentially depends. Whence St. Thomas in *De Spiritualibus Creaturis*, art. 1, ad 24, says that when genus is said to be taken from the matter, that is not to be understood to concern prime matter but to be concerned with the imperfect and, with respect to specific being, material being which it re-

---

[46] *Disputation XXXV, De Immateriali Substantia Creata*, Numbers 34 through 36, *op. cit.* (note 1), Vol. 26.

ceives through the form, just as "to be an animal" is imperfect with respect to "being a man," and each is from the soul. Whence it happens that matter, properly speaking, is not the principle of genus except through an analogy and proportion, as we have said. The form seems to have something more with respect to some difference, since it is its proper root—something which is true not only of the ultimate but also of the subalternate differences. However, a form is not entirely in its genus, if matter be excluded; because every natural form is its act and from it as such the difference is taken, hence matter is always included in some way in such a difference.

6. *Material substances agree univocally with immaterial substances.* There is no lack of those who concede the sequel to the second argument, namely, that there is found no genus common to things not having common matter or matter of the same nature, as was cited above. But this rests upon no reasonable basis, since, as we have shown, composition of genus and species is not absurd for finite things, even if they either consist of no physical matter at all or merely consist of a matter of another type from the matter of these inferiors. Again, it is not absurd for them to have univocal agreement or similarity with these inferiors, as is established in the case of the concept of substance, which when considered according to its precise notion, equally applies to integral material and immaterial substances, and to terrestrial as well as celestial ones. Therefore the argument is answered by our denying the sequel; for in the first place what pertains to celestial and terrestrial bodies: even though we grant that their matters be different in species, since they will still agree in the genus of that matter, there will be no inconvenience in there being one genus common to these bodies, taken from these in its own way, not only insofar as they are substances, but also insofar as they are bodies. What pertains to immaterial substances: they agree univocally with the lower substances under the aspect of "being through themselves" or "subsisting in a substantial nature"; whence they can have a common genus, not taken from the proper matter, but taken from the whole nature with regard to its indetermined aspect, as has been said. Nor does the dictum of Aristotle, "the corruptible and incorruptible differ in genus" conflict with this truth, since as St. Thomas, Alexander of Hales, and others explain him, both here and in 5 *Metaphysics*, text 33, this is not to be interpreted as referring to the logical genus or to the metaphysical genus which is considered through agreement in some formal unity, but is to be interpreted as referring to the physical genus which is matter itself; more about that interpretation below, dis. 39, sec. 3. The third reason has been dismissed by what has already been said.

[123]

MEDIAEVAL PHILOSOPHICAL TEXTS IN TRANSLATION

Translation #1: "Grosseteste: On Light"
by Clare Riedl-Trans.
This treatise is significant as an introduction to an influential thinker and man of science of the Middle Ages.

Translation #2: "St. Augustine: Against the Academicians"
by Sister Mary Patricia, R.S.M.-Trans.
Augustine aims to prove that man need not be content with mere probability in the realm of knowledge.

Translation #3: "Pico Della Mirandola: Of Being and Unity"
by Victor M. Hamm-Trans.
In this work Pico tried to discover the genuine thought of Plato and Aristotle on being and unity.

Translation #4: "Francis Suarez: On the Various Kinds of Distinction"
by Cyril Vollert, S.J.-Trans.
Suarez propounds his theory on distinctions, a point of capital importance for a grasp of Suarezian metaphysics.

Translation #5: "St. Thomas Aquinas: On Spiritual Creatures"
by Mary C. Fitzpatrick-Trans.
This book falls into two general divisions: an introduction and the translation from the Latin.

Translation #6: "Meditations of Guigo"
by John J. Jolin, S.J.-Trans.
A series of reflections by Guigo, 12th century Prior of the hermitage Charterhouse.

Translation #7: "Giles of Rome: Theorems on Existence and Essence"
by Michael V. Murray, S.J.-Trans.
An essay dealing with the *a priori* deductions of being and its conditions.

Translation #8: "John of St. Thomas: Outlines of Formal Logic"
by Francis C. Wade, S.J.-Trans.
A standard English translation of the Logic of John of St. Thomas.

Translation #9: "Hugh of St. Victor: Soliloquy in the Earnest Money of the Soul"
Kevin Herbert-Trans.
The purpose of the work is to direct the soul toward a true love of self, an attitude which is identical with a love of God.

Translation #10: "St. Thomas Aquinas: On Charity"
by Lottie Kendzierski-Trans.
This treatise is significant as an expression of St. Thomas' discussion on the virtue of charity in itself, its object, subject, order, precepts, and principal act.

Translation #11: "Aristotle: On Interpretation-Commentary by St. Thomas and Cajetan"
Jean T. Oesterle-Trans.
This translation will be of particular value to teachers and students of logic.

Translation #12: "Desiderius Erasmus of Rotterdam: On Copia of Words and Ideas"
by Donald B. King and H. David Rix-Trans.
One of the most popular and influential books of the 16th century is made available here for the first time in English.

Translation #13: "Peter of Spain: Tractatus Syncategorematum and Selected Anonymous Treatises"
by Joseph P. Mullally and Roland Houde-Trans.
The first English translation of these tracts now makes it possible for scholars of logic to better appreciate the continuity of Formal Logic.

Translation #14: "Cajetan: Commentary on St. Thomas Aquinas' On Being and Essence"
by Lottie Kendzierski and Francis C. Wade, S.J.-Trans.
A basic understanding of the relation between Cajetan and St. Thomas.

Translation #15: "Suarez: Disputation VI, On Formal and Universal Unity"
by James F. Ross-Trans.
The study of late mediaeval philosophy and the decline of scholasticism.

Translation #16: "St. Thomas, Sieger de Brabant, St. Bonaventure: On the Eternity of the World"
by Cyril Vollert, S.J., Lottie Kendzierski, Paul Byrne-Trans.
A combined work bringing together the writings of three great scholars on the philosophical problem of the eternity of the world.

Translation #17: "Geoffrey of Vinsauf: Instruction in the Method and Art of Speaking and Versifying"
by Roger P. Parr–Trans.
This text, of one of the most important mediaeval literary theorists, is here for the first time translated into English.

Translation #18: "Liber De Pomo: The Apple, or Aristotle's Death"
by Mary F. Rousseau–Trans.
A significant item in the history of mediaeval thought, never previously translated into English from the Latin.

Translation #19: "St. Thomas Aquinas: On the Unity of the Intellect Against the Averroists"
by Beatrice H. Zedler–Trans.
This is a polemical treatise that St. Thomas wrote to answer a difficult problem confronting his times.

Translation #20: "The Universal Treatise of Nicholas of Autrecourt"
by Leonard L. Kennedy C.S.B., Richard E. Arnold, S.J. and Arthur E. Millward, A.M.
This treatise gives an indication of the deep philosophical skepticism at the University of Paris in the mid-fourteenth century.

Translation #21 "Pseudo-Dionysius Aeropagite: The Divine Names and Mystical Theology"
by John D. Jones–Trans.
Among the most important works in the transition from later Greek to Medieval thought.

Translation #22 "Matthew of Vendôme: Ars Versificatoria (The Art of the Versemaker)"
by Roger P. Parr–Trans.
The Text of this, the earliest of the major treatises of the *Artest Poetical* is here translated in toto with special emphasis given to maintaining the full nature of the complete original text.

Translation #23 "Suarez on Individuation, Metaphysical Disputation V: Individual Unity and its Principle"
by Jorge J.E. Gracia–Trans.
Gracia discusses in masterful detail the main positions on the problem of individuation developed in the Middle Ages and offers his own original view.

Translation #24 Francis Suarez: On the Essence of the Finite Being as Such, on the Existence of That Essence and Their Distinction.
by Norman J. Wells–Trans.
From the Latin "De Essentia Entis Ut Tale Est, Et De Illius Esse, Eorumque Distinctione, by Francisco Suarez, S.J. in the 16th Century.

Translation #25 "The Book of Causes (Liber De Causis)"
by Dennis Brand–Trans.
One of the central documents in the dossier on Neo-Platonism in the Middle Ages. Translated from the 13th Century Latin.

Translation #26 "Giles of Rome: Errores Philosophorum"
by John O. Riedl–Trans.
A previously little-known work that bears new attention due to revived interest in mediaeval studies. Author makes compilation of exact source references of the Errores philosophorum, Aristotelis, Averrois, Avicennae, Algazelis, Alinkdi, Rabbi Moysis, which were contrary to the Christian Faith.

Translation #27 "St. Thomas Aquinas: Questions on the Soul"
by James H. Robb–Trans.
The last major text of St. Thomas on Man as Incarnate spirit. In this last of his major texts on what it means to be a human being, St. Thomas develops a new and unique approach to the question. The introduction discusses and summarizes the key themes of St. Thomas' philosophical anthropology.

James H. Robb, Ph.D. is editor of the Mediaeval Philosophical Texts in Translation.

Copies of this translation and the others in the series are obtainable from:
Marquette University Press
Marquette University
Milwaukee, Wisconsin 53233, U.S.A.

Publishers of:

| • Mediaeval Philosophical Texts in Translation | • Père Marquette Theology Lectures | • St. Thomas Aquinas Lectures |